Malcolm Johnson qualified as a solicitor in 1994. He works for Hudgell Solicitors as a Senior Solicitor. He is a solicitor advocate, who has represented his clients at trial, inquests, in the Upper Tier Tribunal and the Court of Appeal.

Malcolm is a Fellow of the Association of Personal Injury Lawyers and a member of the Law Society's Personal Injury Panel. He is also the co-ordinator of APIL's Child Injury Special Interest Group. He is the author of "Child Abuse Compensation Claims" published by Jordans. He has written numerous articles in the legal press. Malcolm also advises Coram Voice, a London based charity who support children in care. He is one of the authors of "Complaints for Advocates" published by Pavilion.

A Practical Guide to Prison Injury Claims

A Practical Guide to Prison Injury Claims

Malcolm Johnson – Solicitor Advocate

Law Brief Publishing

Published 2019 by Law Brief Publishing, an imprint of Law Brief Publishing Ltd
30 The Parks
Minehead
Somerset
TA24 8BT

www.lawbriefpublishing.com

Paperback: 978-1-912687-30-5

PREFACE

When I sat down to write this book, it was very clear to me that prisons and detention centres operate very much in their own world, under a complex and voluminous set of rules and regulations. Yet, as case after case has shown, their capacity to perpetrate or allow damage to those whom they incarcerate is very great indeed. This book is concerned with personal injury, but injury claims frequently go hand in hand with other types of claims, such as wrongful detention and human rights and so these are also considered in some detail. This book cannot explain the entirety of prison law, and there are books to which I refer in Chapter One, which undertake that task admirably. The problem with these books (as with any book) is that the law has moved swiftly onwards since their publication and there are now new rules and regulations that cover prisons.

What this book tries to do is introduce personal injury practitioners to the world of prisons, and explain some of those rules and regulations, as well as where to obtain their sources. Bringing a claim against what is essentially a closed society is often very difficult indeed. The book is intended to help practitioners master the basic principles of identifying the Defendant whom they are suing, the evidence that they need to collect, the procedure for bringing a claim and the different types of claim that can be made by reference to reported cases. I hope that practitioners find it helpful, and I welcome their comments.

The stated law in this book is believed to be correct and up-to-date as at the 30th June 2019.

Malcolm Johnson
July 2019

ACKNOWLEDGEMENTS

Malcolm is grateful to Andrew Petherbridge, Head of Civil Liberties at Hudgells for his help in producing this book.

CONTENTS

CHAPTER ONE
AN INTRODUCTION TO INJURY CLAIMS IN PRISON

1.1 What this book covers

The concept of a prison in English law encompasses a whole host of different institutions, run by different organisations, both public and private. As we see below, there are places where adults or children are detained, but not all are called prisons. In this book, I have tried to cover the prison system run by HM Prison and Probation Service, which for brevity's sake we call the Prison Service. Some mention is made of probation services, but the focus is on those who are or have been detained in prisons. I have also covered very briefly the detention system that exists for children and people whose immigration status is at issue. I have not covered injuries or death in police custody.

This book is concerned mainly with injury claims brought by both prisoners and the people who work in prisons. As we will see in Chapters Four and Five, claims by prisoners frequently rely on different causes of action, such as negligence, trespass to the person, misfeasance in public office and human rights.

The purpose of this book is to try and give practitioners an idea as to how the prison system works, and how to build a personal injury claim in circumstances that can be very challenging indeed. As a number of reports and court judgments on the prison system have shown, prisons can be highly secretive places, cut off from the outside world, where abuse and corruption can flourish unchecked. It is generally accepted by the courts that prisoners are highly vulnerable people, who require a high degree of protection.

1.2 Getting background information about prisons and their practices

There are a number of reports and research papers published by various organisations, which whilst they are unlikely to provide corroborative evidence in a personal injury claim, can be extremely useful to read as a way of understanding how the system was working or should have worked at any particular time. They also make reference to the documents commonly used by the Prison Service to record incidents or assess risk.

The Howard League for Penal Reform's website https://howard-league.org/ contains a huge amount of information on what is happening in prisons. The League and other charities also publish online research and reports. For instance, one recent publication by the Howard League, "*Preventing prison suicide*" contains references to the suicide prevention methods that the Prison Service uses including "ACCT" (Assessment, Care in Custody and Teamwork). We look at ACCT again in Chapter Four.

There are also the reports published by the Prisons and Probations Ombudsman ("PPO") – https://www.ppo.gov.uk/ whose work we examine in more detail later in this book. The PPO carries out independent investigations into deaths and complaints in prison. His 2017 to 2018 Annual Report has a section entitled "*Investigating fatal incidents*" which discusses the way in which ACCT is operated in prisons, and it refers to the Guidance on ACCT procedures set out in Prison Service Instruction (PSI) 64/2011 "*Management of prisoners at risk of harm to self, to others and from others (Safer Custody)*".

The PPO also publishes the results of his investigations into complaints that are brought by prisoner, including fatal incidents (after an inquest has taken place), as well as a series of "Learning lessons reports" on a variety of prison issues, such as segregation and sexual abuse in prison. From time to time, the PPO is invited to carry out investigations into matters that fall outside his normal remit although the most recent report on the website dates back to 2008.

The Office of the Chief Coroner section of the Courts and Tribunal Judiciary website, https://www.judiciary.uk/related-offices-and-bodies/office-chief-coroner/key-cases/ contains key cases where decisions of the Coroner have been challenged by way of judicial review. These include deaths in custody. This section of the website also contains reports made by Coroners pursuant to Regulation 28 of the Coroners (Investigations) Regulations 2013, which are in effect recommendations made to the authorities to prevent further deaths.

HM Inspectorate of Prisons ("HMIP") is an independent inspectorate which reports on the conditions and treatment of prisoners – https://www.justiceinspectorates.gov.uk/hmiprisons/. It publishes reports and recommendations for improvement in its reports. During the inspection of prisons, HMIP can identify significant concerns and write to the Home Office providing notification of the significant concerns and the reasons for those concerns. These arc published on the website as "*Urgent Notifications.*"

The Independent Advisory Panel on Deaths in Custody provides independent advice and expertise to the Ministerial Board on Deaths in Custody. It covers deaths that occur in prisons, in or following police custody, immigration detention, the deaths of residents of approved premises and the deaths of those detained under the Mental Health Act 1983.

The IAP's website can be found at :- http://iapdeathsincustody.independent.gov.uk/.

1.3 Recommended reading

Prison law is a subject of itself, and the prison system is very complicated with its own procedures and practices. To help navigate the maze, there are three excellent books on the subject of prison law, which are :-

- 'Prisoners – Law and Practice' – Simon Creighton and Hamish Arnott – Legal Action Group 2009
- 'Prison Law – Fourth Edition' – Stephen Livingstone, Tim Owen QC and Alison Macdonald – Oxford 2008
- 'Inquests – A Practitioner's Guide' – Leslie Thomas QC, Adam Straw, Daniel Machover and Danny Friedman QC – Legal Action Group 2014

Although the first two books are at least a decade old and some of the law and the prison procedures that they describe have changed, they are well worth purchasing. They are written by highly experienced and eminent practitioners and they provide an in-depth examination of the legal basis on which prisons function, the way in which they are run and the various types of legal claims that prisoners bring, including injury claims.

Chapters 18 and 19 of 'Inquests – A Practitioners Guide' are more up to date and incorporate a very helpful section on deaths in prison as well as deaths under restraint. It is mandatory reading for anyone contemplating representing the family of a deceased prisoner at an inquest.

Chapter Five of the 'Immigration and Asylum Handbook' published by the Law Society provides a short but very helpful guide to immigration detention centres.

1.4 Charities that support prisoners

There are a number of charities that work tirelessly to support prisoners and which campaign to reform prison law. They can provide very useful sources of information as well as up-to-date news on what is happening within the Prison Service. The following are four of these charities :-

The Howard League – https://howardleague.org/

The Howard League for Penal Reform is the oldest penal reform charity in the UK. It was established in 1866 and is named after John Howard, one of the first prison reformers. Over the years it has run a number of successful campaigns on behalf of both children and adults in the prison system. It publishes the Howard Journal of Crime and Justice. They also bring legal cases, sometimes in their own name or through interventions, to help shape the law.

The Prisoners' Advice Service ("PAS") – http://www.prisonersadvice.org.uk/

PAS is an independent charity founded by a number of organisations including the Prison Reform Trust, and the Howard League to offer free legal advice and support to adult prisoners throughout England and Wales. They produce a quarterly Prisoners' Legal Rights Bulletin (available by subscription), in order to share updates on key Prison Law cases with prisoners, human rights organisations and legal professionals. This Bulleting also provides information about new legislation and cases, new Prison Service Instructions and Orders, and commentary on cases that have gone before the Prisons and Probations Ombudsman.

PAS also produces a series of Self-Help Toolkits and Information Sheets on their website, which are designed to assist prisoners with various legal issues. These Toolkits provide very useful information on a variety of different issues, such as Category A prisoners and disciplinary offences committed in prison.

There is also a 'Links' page on their website with links to other charities.

The Prison Reform Trust – http://www.prisonreformtrust.org.uk/

This is an independent UK charity working to create a just, humane and effective penal system. They do this by inquiring into the workings of the system; informing prisoners, staff and the wider public; and by influencing Parliament, government and officials towards reform.

The Prison Advice and Care Trust ("PACT") – https://www.prisonadvice.org.uk/

PACT is a national charity that provides support to prisoners, people with convictions, and their families. They support people to make a fresh start, and minimise the harm that can be caused by imprisonment to people who have committed offences, to families and to communities.

INQUEST – https://www.inquest.org.uk/

INQUEST provides expertise on state related deaths and their investigation to bereaved people, lawyers, advice and support agencies, the media and parliamentarians. It publishes "Inquest Law" three times a year, which contains summaries of cases and examines various issues. It also publishes reports on deaths in prison. One example is "*Stolen Lives and Missed Opportunities – The deaths of young adults and children in prison*" (March 2015).

1.5 InsideTime

This is the national newspaper for prisoners and detainees. It can be found online at https://insidetime.org/insideinformation-home/ and it is a comprehensive guide covering all UK prisons and prison related issues. The service is designed and is maintained with input from former prisoners and their families. All prison information is gathered directly from each individual establishment and a range of Legal Factsheets provided by various legal specialists provide simple explanations to prison law and other legal issues. It also provides an extensive glossary to the many terms used in the Prison Service, at https://insidetime.org/glossary/.

CHAPTER TWO
HOW THE PRISON SERVICE WORKS

2.1 The structure of the Prison Service

At present, HM Prison and Probation Services ("HMPPS") is the government agency that runs the prison and probation services. Before the 1st April 2017, HMPPS was the National Offender Manager Service ("NOMS") and obviously references to NOMS will appear in documents, reports and caselaw from before that date.

In their own words, HMPPS carry out sentences given by the courts, in custody and the community, and rehabilitate people in their care through education and employment. Their functions include rehabilitation services for people leaving prison, managing private sector prisons, and providing services such as the prisoner escort service and electronic tagging. They also oversee the custody of children and young people in secure training centres, young offender institutions, and secure accommodation.

HMPPS does its work through two other agencies, HM Prison Service and the National Probation Service. The National Probation Service was established by the Criminal Justice and Court Services Act 2000. It supervises high-risk offenders released into the community and works alongside Community Rehabilitation Companies that manage low and medium risk offenders. At the time of writing, the government intends to bring back the supervision of all offenders in England and Wales under public control from December 2020.

Probation means that a person is still serving out their sentence but they are not in prison. A person who is a serving a community sentence, or who has been released from prison on licence or on parole, will generally be put on probation. Whilst on probation, that person may have to do unpaid work, complete an education or training course, get treatment for addiction and have regular meetings with an offender manager.

Prior to 2007, prisons were run by the Secretary of State for the Home Office, or more simply the Home Office. They were then transferred to the Ministry of Justice which makes the Ministry the effective Defendant in most cases of injury in prison, unless the prison is privately run.

Practitioners should bear in mind that Rule 6.10 and Practice Direction 66 of the Civil Procedure Rules require a Claimant to serve proceedings against a government department on its nominated solicitors, the Treasury Solicitors (now the Government Legal Department).

2.2 Prisons for adults and their categories

Most adult prisoners are housed in various prisons up and down the country, which are run either by the Prison Service or by private companies. InsideTime publishes a very useful search facility for prisons at https://insidetime.org/visits/ as well an immigration removal centres at https://insidetime.org/irc-immigration-removal-centres/.

In England and Wales, prisoners are categorised based on the risk of escape, harm to the public, if they were to escape and their threat to the control and stability of a prison

Male prisons are organised into 4 categories :-

Category A

These are high security prisons. They house male prisoners who, if they were to escape, pose the most threat to the public, the police or national security.

Category B

These prisons are either local or training prisons. Local prisons house prisoners that are taken directly from court in the local area (sentenced or on remand), and training prisons hold long-term and high-security prisoners.

Category C

These prisons are training and resettlement prisons; most prisoners are located in a Category C. They provide prisoners with the opportunity to develop their own skills so they can find work and resettle back into the community on release.

Category D – open prisons

These prisons have minimal security and allow eligible prisoners to spend most of their day away from the prison on licence to carry out work, education or for other resettlement purposes. Open prisons only house prisoners that have been risk-assessed and deemed suitable for open conditions.

2.3 Young Offender Institutions and Secure Training Centres

Young Offender Institutions are for boys aged 15 – 17 and young adult men aged 18 – 21. There are five young offender institutions in England & Wales, which are Cookham Wood, Feltham, Parc, Werrington and Wetherby. They provide education and training for inmates.

Secure Training Centres provide more specialist education and training than YOIs. There are three in England and Wales, Medway, Oakhill and Rainsbrook. Medway and Oakhill are run by G4S. MTCnovo took over the running of Rainsbrook in May 2016.

Youth Offender Institutions and Secure Training Centres are overseen by the Prison Service. The Youth Justice Board decides where children who are remanded or sentenced to custody are placed.

2.4 Secure children's homes or secure accommodation

Secure children's homes or secure accommodation are specialist placements authorised to care for children (aged between 10 and 17 years) in a locked setting. This restriction of liberty is not permitted in other types of children's homes and there are legal safeguards to make sure that secure accommodation is only used where specific criteria are met.

There are two main pathways into a secure placement: the youth justice system or when a child is taken into care under the Children Act 1989.

There are four secure accommodation units in England. All but one are operated by individual local authorities. They are the preferred option for custodial sentences for children, who receive individual attention and support from well training staff and they are viewed as considerably more therapeutic than Young Offender Institutions and Secure Training Centres (both of which do provide education as well). Unsurprisingly it is very difficult to get a child into secure accommodation and they are very expensive.

2.5 Immigration Removal Centres and Short-Term Holding Facilities

The Home Office oversees the UK's immigration system. People who enter this country illegally or those who are found to be living here illegally can be detained in detention centres known as Immigration Removal Centres or Short-Term Holding Facilities pending possible deportation. Foreign people who have committed serious crimes and who are liable to be deported from the country may be already held in prisons.

There are nine Immigration Removal Centres in the United Kingdom. Harmondsworth, near Heathrow, is the largest detention centre in Europe, holding up to 630 people at any one time. Residential Short-Term Holding Facilities can hold people for up to seven days. There are three of these facilities: in Manchester, in Northern Ireland, and in Bedfordshire. There is also a unit for families within Tinsley House, near Gatwick Airport, which operates as a Short-Term Holding Facility.

The Home Office contracts out the management of detention facilities to private providers, and to the Prison Service.

2.6 The Prison Act 1952

Section 1 of the Prison Act 1952 gives the government powers and jurisdiction over prisons subject to any other provisions of the Act.

Section 4(1) provides:

> *"The Secretary of State shall have the general superintendence of prisons, and shall make the contracts and the other acts necessary for the maintenance of prisons and maintenance of prisoners."*

Section 5A provides for the appointment of a Chief Inspector of Prisons who reports to the government.

Section 13(1) provides that prisoner is deemed to be in the legal custody of the governor of the prison. Subsection (2) identifies the circumstances and locations in which that custody will arise.

Section 47(1) of the Act enables the government to make rules for the regulation and management of prisons. These are the Prison Rules 1999.

The House of Lords decision in ***R v Deputy Governor of Parkhurst, ex parte Leech [1988] 1 AC 533*** and the decision of the Divisional Court in ***R v Deputy Governor of Parkhurst, ex parte Hague [1992] 1 AC 588*** confirm that the Prison Service is subject to judicial review.

2.7 The Prison Rules 1999

The management of prisons and the treatment of most adult prisoners are subject to the Prison Rules 1999, which are made by the government under the Prison Act 1952. These regulations/rules provide for the training and treatment of prisoners. For example, Regulation 3 states that the purpose of the training and treatment of convicted prisoners shall be to encourage and assist them to lead a good and useful life. Rule 45 is the rule under which a prisoner may be segregated or removed from association with other prisoners for reasons of maintaining good order or discipline or in the prisoner's own interest. Regulation 49 deals with the use of restraint on prisoners. Rule 51 deals with offences against discipline.

2.8 Prison Governors and Independent Monitoring Boards

Section 6 of the Prison Act 1952 requires the Secretary of State to appoint a Board of Visitors for each prison, who make frequent visits and hear any complaints. These are now Independent Monitoring Boards.

Section 7 requires that every prison shall have a governor, a chaplain and a medical officer and such other officers as may be necessary. Prison officers have different grades according to their seniority, and the most senior prison officer is the governor, of whom in any one prison there may be seven or so.

Prison governors manage the security of prisons, remand centres, and young offenders' institutions. They are the higher operational managers in the prison system. They may be responsible for a particular "wing" or section of a prison rather than the whole prison.

Under the Prison Act 1952, it is a requirement that every prison is monitored by an Independent Monitoring Board. The Board's members are appointed by the government from volunteer members of the community, in which the prison is situated. A member of the board has access, at any time, to every part of the prison and to every prisoner. They can also interview any prisoner out of the sight and hearing of officers.

2.9 Prison Service Orders ("PSOs") Instructions ("PSIs") and Policy Frameworks

2.9.1 Introduction

The 1952 Act and the 1999 Rules are only a framework. There are a huge number of rules, regulations and guidelines by which prisons are run, and which are set out in documents known as Prison Service Orders, Prison Service Instructions and since September 2018, Policy Frameworks.

These documents have no legal status but they contain a great deal of detail about how the Prison Service is expected to behave in certain situations, the kind of records that may be available and they are key to understanding how the system was supposed to work at any given time. A serving prisoner, particularly one who has been in the system for some time may actually have some appreciation of how the system is supposed to work and certainly they may be able to give coherent evidence of what actually happened in terms of official action. In any claim, these guidance documents are bound to be relevant evidence as to what the Prison Service was expected to do in any given situation.

As we will see below, PSOs, PSIs and Policy Frameworks cross refer to other documents in the overall system, and which are relevant to the same issues. They will also contain information as to when they came into force, and when they expire, what documents they replace and when they have been updated or revised.

PSOs, PSIs and Policy Frameworks are published on the government's website, and we set out the addresses below. There is a numerical index and a subject index for PSOs. The numerical index confirms which PSOs have been cancelled or replaced by a PSI but it is not clear when the subject index was issued or whether it is up to date. There is also a chronological index for PSIs although this only goes up to the beginning of 2017. There are only a few Policy Frameworks issued since September 2018.

There are also Probation Instructions at https://www.justice.gov.uk/offenders/probation-instructions .

Making a claim purely based on breach of these statutory rules and regulations is generally not permitted. In ***R v. Home Office ex parte Hague and Weldon [1992] 1 AC 58*** the first Claimant made a claim for false imprisonment and breach of statutory duty for being held in solitary confinement. The second Claimant, Mr Weldon brought a claim for assault and false imprisonment in which he alleged he had been beaten up by prison staff and left inside a strip cell without lawful authority. When the case reached the House of Lords, the issue was whether the existing prison legislation gave rise to a private law claim for breach of statutory duty. The House of Lords decided that the fact that a particular part of the statutory provisions was designed to protect individuals was not a reason to confer a private law action for breach of those provisions.

Nonetheless, a court dealing with an injury claim against a prison will be interested to know precisely what the Prison Rules and the various regulations and guidance documents (Prison Service Orders, Instructions and Policy Frameworks) issued by the Prison Service say about a particular situation, in order to establish where liability lies. In Chapter Five we examine cases where the courts have examined the way in which statutes have changed the responsibilities for healthcare in prison, and made findings of liability based partly on what those statutes say.

By way of example, in ***Thompson v Home Office [2001] EWCA Civ 331*** a prisoner was attacked with a razor blade and he claimed against the Prison Service on the basis that the for providing and recovering razor blades was negligent. The Home Office said that they had followed their own guidelines about razors and their system was such that, balancing all relevant considerations, they discharged their duty of care. In the Court of Appeal, the Home Office submitted that the lawfulness of these guidelines was not challenged. Lord Justice said that this submission muddled public law and private law duties. There was no dispute but that, in the present case, the prison authorities owed the claimant a private law duty to take reasonable care for his safety. The fact that the Home Office issued guidelines was a relevant starting point, but no more, to the question of whether the prison authorities were in breach of that duty.

2.9.2 Prison Service Orders

PSOs were issued up until the 31st July 2009. They are long-term mandatory instructions which are intended to last indefinitely and as such do not have an expiry date. PSOs remain in force until replaced by a PSI or cancelled.

Examples of PSOs are :-

PSO 1600 – use of force
PSO 1700 – segregation
PSO 2855 – guidance on the management of prisoners with disabilities.
PSO 3050 – prisoners' health
PSO 3550 – clinical services for substance misusers
PSO 8805 – identification of prison officers

PSO 1600 is the Prison Service's policy covering the use of force. It details the circumstances in which force can be used and the framework for justifying the use of force. It covers not only Control and Restraint techniques but also de-escalation skills, personal safety techniques and the use of batons.

PSO 1700 relates to segregation. The PSO is made up of a series of documents beginning with a letter from the National Offender Management Service dated the 4th September 2015 setting out a revised policy on segregation reviews.

PSO 3050 – Continuity of Healthcare for Prisoners contains guidance to improve the continuity of healthcare received by prisoners. It includes guidance on reception, transfer and discharge of prisoners, with particular focus on those with ongoing health needs. At paragraph 2.5 it sets out a new format for the clinical record (formerly Inmate Medical Record) for use in prisons

PSOs can be found at http://www.justice.gov.uk/offenders/psos .

2.9.3 Prison Service Instructions

Prior to the introduction of Policy Frameworks, all Prison Service operating instructions were published as PSIs, and they were issued year since 1997. All PSIs have a date from which they are effective. More recent PSIs from 2016 onwards have no expiry date but earlier PSIs do.

It appears that despite having an expiry date, some PSIs are still current. One example is PSI 30/2013 Incentives and Earned Privileges, which despite having an expiry date of the 4th September 2017, was revised on the 23rd January 2019 and it is still referred to in PSI 16/2015 – Adult Safeguarding in Prisons which has an expiry date of the 31st March 2019.

The following is a list of PSI examples.

- PSI 04/2018 – Records, Information Management and Retention Policy
- PSI 01/2018 – Home Detention Curfew
- PSI 02/2018 – Post incident care for members of Prison Service staff

- PSI 05/2018 – Prison Discipline Procedures (Adjudications) – Annex E contains a very helpful list of short summaries of challenges made by prisoners to the adjudication system.
- PSI 31/2015 – Managing Litigation Claims
- PSI 16/2015 – Adult Safeguarding in Prisons
- PSI 20/2015 – Cell Sharing Risk Assessment
- PSI 07/2015 – Early Days in Custody
- PSI 06/2015 – National Policy, Organisation and Summary Arrangements for the Management of Health and Safety
- PSI 15/2014 – Investigations and learning following incidents of serious self-harm or serious assaults
- PSI 64/2011 – Management of Prisoners at Risk of Harm to Self, to Others and From Others (Safer Custody)
- PSI 52/2010 – early days in custody

PSI 06/2015 relates to the Prison Service's Health and Safety Management Arrangements as required by the Health and Safety at Work etc. Act 1974 and subsidiary legislation and it contains a list of associated documents. The following are some of these :-

- PSI 36/2015 – Health and Safety Arrangements for Workplace Inspection sets out the minimum requirements for workplace and work area health and safety inspection.
- PSI 37/2015 – NOMS Health and Safety Arrangements for Risk Assessment creates a framework and program to collect risk assessments the Prison Service's own Health and Safety Management Software (Rivo Safeguard or "*Rivo*").

- PSI 38/2015 – Health and Safety Arrangements for the Monitoring and Measurement of Health and Safety Performance summarises the key duties to be undertaken by staff and managers and the systems that operate to monitor, and report on, the effectiveness of the Prison Service's health and safety management system.

PSI 31/2015 – Managing Litigation Claims sets out the arrangements for the management of litigation claims, including both private law (i.e. personal injury) claims and judicial reviews. It is obviously mandatory reading for anyone setting out on a litigation claim against the Prison Service.

Paragraph 1.12 of the PSI makes it clear that it does not apply to litigation or inquests arising out of a death in custody. This kind of litigation is handled in accordance with Chapter 12 of PSI 64/2011, whilst claims relating to investigations under Articles 2 or 3 of the European Convention of Human Rights should be handled under PSI 15/2014.

Paragraph 3.2 of the PSI contains the following principle :-

> *"NOMS defends all claims robustly, as far as the evidence allows. This includes those that give rise to important points of principle. NOMS will settle cases only if there are compelling reasons why this is appropriate in all circumstances of the particular case. NOMS will consider the best possible outcome for the taxpayer and seek to discourage a compensation culture. Unsuccessful litigants will be pursued for NOMS' legal costs where possible. If there is evidence that the claim has not be brought in good faith, enquiries will be made and action taken, if appropriate."*

Annex C of PSI 31/2015 sets out the criteria in which certain claims will be sent to its claims handler, Gallagher Bassett and others (i.e. high profile, complex or large quantum cases) to the Government Legal Department.

Finally, PSI 31/2015 contains the kinds of documents that are routinely released to Claimants in litigation. We consider these in more detail in Chapter Three.

PSI 16/2015 – Adult Safeguarding in Prisons relates to the protection of adult prisoners from abuse or neglect. It refers to other PSIs and PSOs, some of which are :-

- PSI 07/2015 Early Days in Custody states the mandatory requirement for all prisoners to be "assessed for potential harm to themselves, to others and from others" on reception into custody, and explains that this must be done using all available information, as well as by interviewing the prisoner.

- PSI 30/2013 Incentives and Earned Privileges (IEP) describes how positive behaviour, including helping other prisoners, is encouraged.

- PSI 64/2011 Safer Custody sets out how prisons are required to address issues of violence in prison in all its forms, including physical and sexual assaults.

- PSO 1700 Segregation sets out the procedures for segregating prisoners for the purposes of maintaining good order or discipline and/or for their own protection.

- PSI 17/2015 Prisoners Assisting Other Prisoners describes the parameters for this form of peer support, including the measures that must be in place to ensure that it does not result in abuse or neglect.

PSIs can be found at http://www.justice.gov.uk/offenders/psis

2.9.4 Policy Frameworks

Policy Frameworks began to replace PSIs in September 2018 although many PSOs and PSIs remain in force. They are intended to simplify the current PSO and PSI system.

The first of these Policy Frameworks is the policy entitled "Manage the Custodial Sentence Policy Framework". This describes the minimum mandatory requirements which are needed to deliver the custodial sentence and case manage those in custody from reception to end of supervision post release. The core requirements of the Offender Management in Custody ("OMiC") model and the policy for custodial sentence planning have been incorporated into this Policy Framework.

We need to say a brief word about OMiC. This is mentioned in the above Policy Framework at paragraph 1.3 :-

> *"The OMiC Model provides the framework to co-ordinate and sequence an individual's journey through custody and post release. The OMiC model places prisoners and the development of rehabilitation cultures in prisons at the heart of offender management processes and supports the reduction of re-offending in custody and the community, the rehabilitation culture and re-integration into the community."*

The OMiC model was first introduced by the Government in 2005 as a new and unified approach to offender management. It is the way in which the government seeks to retain and promote best practice developed within prisons and build a rehabilitative culture.

Another example of a Policy Framework is the "Intelligence Collection, Analysis and Dissemination Policy Framework" which sets out the requirements for senior managers in prison establishments and probation teams as to how intelligence should be managed within the Prison Service. It provides a single set of standards for when intelligence can, and should, be used. The Prison and Probation Services use a system called the Offender Assessment System ("OASys") for assessing the risks and needs of an offender.

The Enhanced Behaviour Monitoring ("EBM") Policy Framework provides a mechanism for giving assurance that ongoing risks (e.g. of harm; re-offending, or abscond) are being appropriately identified and managed within open prisons and with relevant residents of women's prisons, and subsequently as individuals are permitted to spend unescorted periods of time away from the prison in the community whilst Released on Temporary Licence ("ROTL").

Policy Frameworks can be found at
https://www.gov.uk/government/collections/prison-probation-policy-frameworks .

2.10 Private prisons and contractors

The Criminal Justice Act 1991 allowed the government to contract out the running of prisons. The private company, G4S now runs some five prisons including one Youth Offender Institution. The other private contractors are Serco and Sodexo.

A list of private prisons can be found at
https://www.justice.gov.uk/about/hmps/contracted-out .

There are also services provided to prisons, such as health care which are provided by private contractors. Since 2013, responsibility for commissioning all healthcare services for prisoners (including drug and alcohol services but excluding emergency and out of hours services) rests with NHS England.

This creates a problem as to who is the correct Defendant. In relation to human rights claims, the contractor of a private prison is carrying out a public function. Section 6(3)(b) of the Human Rights Act 1998 brings within the scope of the Act "*any person certain of whose functions are functions of a public nature.*" Consequently, human rights proceedings can be brought against the private contractor directly.

Similarly, an action based on assault by a prison officer employed by a private contractor, or an act of negligence on the part of the private contractor would be brought against the contractor.

However, great care needs to be taken here and an active enquiry needs to be undertaken at the beginning of the case as to who might be responsible. The case of ***Razumas v Ministry of Justice [2018] EWHC 215 (QB)*** which we examine in Chapter Five concerned a prisoner who alleged clinical negligence against the Prison Service in circumstances where his health care was provided by private contractors. The court decided that whilst the Ministry of Justice owed him some duty of care to provide health care, it was not wide enough for him to win his case.

2.11 Young Offender Institutions ("YOIs"), Secure Training Centres ("STCs") and Secure Children's Homes

YOIs come under the Young Offenders Institution Rules 2000. These Rules make provision for the management of young offender institutions, including the treatment of inmates, the conduct of young offender institution officers, and the powers and duties of the boards of visitors.

STCs come under the Secure Training Centre Rules 1998.

In relation to Secure children's homes or secure accommodation, the relevant regulations are the Children (Secure Accommodation) Regulations 1991.

Section 25 of the Children Act 1989 allows a local authority to detain a child by using this kind of accommodation. It is used for children who have a history of absconding, who are likely to run away from accommodation which is not secure; and if they do run away, they are either likely to suffer significant harm or harm themselves or someone else.

Section 25 is used very sparingly and there is a general shortage of secure accommodation.

A child who is under 13 years of age cannot be placed in secure accommodation without the prior approval of the Department for Education unless the child is 12 and has been arrested by the police.

The 1991 Regulations provide a comprehensive system for depriving children of their liberty. A child can be detained for a maximum period in accommodation without court authority (regulation 10), and there is a maximum initial period of authorisation by any court (regulation 11). Further periods of detention have to be authorised by a court (regulation 12). There is a prohibition on the use of accommodation for restricting liberty in voluntary homes and registered children's homes and breach thereof (regulation 18).

The Independent Inquiry into Child Sexual Abuse ("IICSA") recently published its findings on the sexual of children in prison :- https://www.iicsa.org.uk/news/inquiry-publishes-report-children-custodial-institutions. Focusing on the period from 2009 to 2017, IICSA concluded that children held in young offender institutions and secure training centres were still not safe from sexual abuse. Information obtained directly from the institutions and authorities showed there were over 1,000 incidents of alleged sexual abuse reported during the relevant period.

2.12 Immigration Detention

Foreign citizens can be detained whilst they await deportation. The Home Office exercises its powers of detention and deportation under a series of Acts, which are :-

- The Immigration Act 1971
- The Nationality, Asylum and Immigration Act 2002

- The UK Borders Act 2007
- The Immigration Rules
- The Immigration (European Economic Area) Regulations 2006
- The Detention Centre Rules 2001

Home Office Guidance entitled "Offender Management" (formerly Chapter 55 of the Home Office document, Enforcement Instructions and Guidance) explains how enforcement works in practice. It also requires that the Home Office promptly provides reasons for detention at its outset, using Form IS91R. A failure to do so renders the detention unlawful. Following the initial detention, regular reviews are necessary, the reasons for which must be given on Form IS93.

A failure to conduct reviews may render detention unlawful although release although if it transpires that the detained person would have been detain in any event, they cannot recover anything more than nominal damages.

CHAPTER THREE
PRISON RECORDS – WHERE TO FIND THE EVIDENCE

3.1 Subject access requests

All subject access requests for prisoners are dealt with by the Informtion Services Division of the Prisoner Service.

Records Manager
Branston Division
Departmental Library and Records Management Service
Building 16, NDC Site
Burton Road, Branston
Burton on Trent
Staffordshire
DE14 3EG

3.2 Reports and Serious Case Reviews

There are any number of reports that are published on particular prisons, which can be helpful to the practitioner, as they identify particular concerns about prisons and particular systems. Sometimes these are generic but they can relate to particular individuals.

The Howard League's news section on their website has a very good list of these reports as they come out, as they respond to them. One example is the Serious Case Review from Medway Safeguarding Children Board's arising from incidents at Medway Secure Training Centre, which came out in January of this year. The Serious Case Review was initiated after a BBC Panorama documentary, broadcast in January 2016, identified abuse of children by staff. It focused on the three-year period from September 2014 to September 2017. The report can be found at :- http://www.mscb.org.uk/

Another is the joint inspection report on Rainsbrook secure training centre in Warwickshire, published in January 2019. The report – produced jointly by Ofsted, the Care Quality Commission and Her Majesty's Inspectorate of Prisons – reveals the findings from an inspection conducted in October. The report can be found at :- https://www.cqc.org.uk/location/RP1Y6

A report from the Prison Service itself or the Prisons and Probation Ombudsman can also provide the necessary evidential ammunition.

None of these reports will bind a court or a Coroner to reach a particular conclusion. What they may do however is persuade the Prison Service to reach a settlement or if not, then they provide a route map to the kind of evidence that is going to support or contradict the Claimant's case.

3.3 Evidence from Case Law

In Chapter Five we examine a number of different cases where prisoners have brought claims against the Prison Services, including claims for negligence. Typically, there will be references to evidential material, and the importance of that material to the case which is why the original judgments repay reading.

So, for instance in ***Thompson v Home Office [2001] EWCA Civ 331*** evidence was produced relevant to the practices of other prisons in relation to the issue of razor blades to prisoners. Ultimately that evidence did not help the Claimant, because the Court of Appeal said that even with a more restrictive practice on razor blades, prisoners would find other ways to assault each other.

An unsuccessful attempt was also made by the Home Office (on appeal) in that case to rely on a single page schedule giving brief statistics of assaults in Young Offender Institutions in the year 1996 to 1997, as well as comparative evidence which was intended to show that the assaults in the prison in question, Swinfen Hall, were in fact lower than in other institutions. The Court of Appeal said that it did not think that the statistical material would be much help. Without much greater detail about each of the institutions, there was little or nothing to be derived from the figures or other additional material.

A final point made by the Court of Appeal was that their judgment on the razor blade regime derived largely from the evidence available in relation to Swinfen Hall in November 1996. The judgment should not be taken as necessarily applying to prisons or Young Offender Institutions generally where different considerations might well apply. Moreover, the policy on razor blades in the Prison Service might well change in the future.

3.4 Expert evidence

In difficult cases, involving the exercise of judgment by prison officer expert evidence may be required. In Chapter Five, we examine the case of ***Stenning v Home Office [2002] EWCA Civ 793*** where the Court of Appeal looked at decisions made by prison officers in Wakefield Prison, dealing with a particular difficult prisoner who had indicated that he would do violence to another prisoner in order to move prisons. The Court of Appeal said that in this case, it would have been quite wrong for any judge to make a finding of negligence in this case without the help of a witness expert in the difficult discipline of risk assessment.

It is not easy to find experts in the field of prisons and other types of detention. It may be best to obtain an expert recommendation from a solicitor who has used such an expert in the past.

A search of the Association of Personal Injury Lawyers' expert database turned up one expert on the issue of restraint. This is the British Self Defence Governing Body – the Centre for Physical Interventions. Their website www.bsdgb.co.uk/ contains useful information about the law of self- defence and restraint. The chairman, Eric Baskind sets out his experience and qualifications.

A search of the Expert Witness Institute turned up several experts, most of whom are medical experts who advise specifically on issues such as deaths in custody and custody medicine.

www.ewi.org.uk/

The UK Register of Expert Witnesses provides a fairly good list of both medical and non medical experts.

www.jspubs.com/expert-witness/si/p/prisons/

The membership of INQUEST provides help in finding suitable experts, although these tend to be medical in nature.

Finally, case law is often the best source of information on a suitable expert. In the case of ***Burn v Ministry of Justice [2012] EWHC 876*** both sides used both prison security experts and medical experts in relation to the issue of what a prison doctor should have done in a particular situation.

3.5 PSI 31/2015 – Managing Litigation Claims

We looked at this PSI briefly in Chapter Two. Apart from setting out the way in which personal injury (and other) claims are handled by the Prison Service it also sets out the evidence that should be provided to the Claimant routinely when a claim is brought. The Letter of Claim should make reference to the Checklists and the documents contained in them.

Annex E contains a "Checklist of Documents Required in Personal Injury Claims." Checklist 1 applies to Public Sector Prisons ("PSP's") and Checklist 2 applies to the National Probation Service ("NPS").

In relation to private prisons, it is suggested that the same Checklists are used for the Letter of Claim.

Very briefly, Checklist 1 contains the following documents :-

- Accident Book Entry
- Wing observation book history for 2 weeks prior to the incident and inmate case notes
- CCTV footage
- Witness statements taken around the time of the incident
- Prison Service Accident, Assault or Near Miss Form and any other accident investigation report.
- Staff report completed at the time.
- HSE Health & Safety Report Form i.e. Form F2508 Report of an Injury and any other communications with HSE or other Statutory Bodies
- Incident Reporting System Report
- Photographs
- Sketch Plan of the site of the accident
- Health & Safety Risk Assessment Record
- Records of similar incidents in the 12 months prior to the incident
- All correspondence with the Claimant and his/her solicitors
- Any reports or recommendations by Ministry of Justice Health & Safety Services
- Minutes of Health and Safety Committee meetings where accident/matter considered
- Record of assessment of suitability and issue of personal protective equipment (PPE)

- Training and/or induction document provided to staff and/or prisoner
- Prisoner's training record F2055C
- Safe System of Work
- Local procedures/policies and any Notices to Staff relating to the type of accident

Checklist 3 contains additional documents required for all slip, trips and fall claims. Checklist 4 contains additional document where plant/machinery is involved. Checklist 5 is for claims brought by prison staff.

Checklist 6 contains additional documents for claims brought by prisoners. Again, briefly these are :-

- Report of Injury to Inmate (F213)
- Inmate Medical Record (now Clinical Record)
- Induction and Training Record for Workplace Accident
- Relevant documentation from inmate's record (Form 2050)
- Mercury Intelligence Reports (IR) and/or Subject Profile as appropriate – the Mercury Intelligence system is used by the Prison Service to record a prisoner's profile, their general history in prison and their criminal record.
- PNOMIS Transfer Reports – the Prison National Offender Management Information System is the centralised computer system by which prison staff manage offenders in public sector prisons. It contains offenders' personal details, offences and case history.
- Cell Sharing Risk Assessments
- Entries from Wing Observation Sheet

- Work, course and/or gym attendance post-incident

Checklist 7 contains additional documents required in assault/control and restraint cases. Checklist 8 is miscellaneous documents.

Annex F contains a checklist of documents required in unlawful detention cases. Annex G is about documents required in Third Party Motor Vehicle Accident Claims, i.e. an injury sustained by a prisoner being transported from one prison to another.

3.6 Records particular to prisoners

The prisoner's file

F2050 – Prisoner's personal record – this is a record of the prisoner's time in prison. It should contain details of his conviction, his sentence and his date of release. There should also be a history of the prisoner's transfers between prisons. The prisoner's disciplinary records should be contained within the F2050 and there may be a F2050A "Information of Special Importance" which will include security information as well as suicide attempts or special medical problems.

Clinical Record (formerly an Inmate Medical Record) – PSO 3050 says that for a prisoner's first reception into custody, an initial assessment of the healthcare needs of all newly received prisoners is undertaken within 24 hours of first reception to identify any existing problems and to plan any subsequent care. A health screen, using another form, a F2169, takes place before the prisoner's first night to primarily detect:

- immediate physical health problems
- immediate mental health problems
- significant drug or alcohol abuse
- risk of suicide and/or self-harm

Other types of record

F213 – Report of Injury to a Prisoner

F213SH – Report of Injury to a Prisoner following self-harm

Disciplinary Proceedings – Annex F to PSI 05/2018 – Prison Discipline Procedures (Adjudications) set out the various forms.

Use of force reports – these are set out in Prison Service Order 1600

Forms to be used following a serious assault – see the Annexes to PSI 15/2014

Forms to be used for prisoners at risk of harm to themselves or others – PSI 64/2011 – Chapter 5 sets out the Assessment, Care in Custody and Teamwork ("ACCT") procedures to be used by the Prison Service for prisoners identified at risk or suicide or self-harm. The ACCT document itself is a series of forms opened in response to concern that an individual in prison is at risk of self-harm or suicide. These include a "Concern and Keep Safe" form, an Immediate Action Plan to ensure the prisoner is safe from harm and a "CAREMAP1" giving detailed and timebound actions aimed at reducing the risk posed by the prisoner.

Segregation forms – these are set out in Prison Service Order 1700

Gatekeeper's Daily Occurrence Book and Wing records – generally the wing in a prison will keep a diary of significant events.

3.7 Evidence held by the Prison Service, the Police and the Crown Prosecution Services that relate to other prisoners and prison staff

In some cases, particularly those involving serious assault against prisoners by either prisoners or staff, the police may be called to the prison and there may be a criminal prosecution. In Chapter Eight we look at cases where the courts have been asked to order disclosure of other types of evidence, such as statement made by other prison officers or inmates, in relation to an incident or that prison officer's or inmate personal record.

However, Checklist 7 to Annex E PSI 31/2015 does provide for a wide variety of documents to be disclosed to the Claimant, including personal information about and statements made by those who are alleged to have committed the assaults. These documents include the history of the behaviour of the victim and the alleged assailants upon the wing prior to the alleged assault, which are contained in records such as the wing records and observation book to be disclosed. It also includes statements given to the police and relevant extracts from the Inmate Personal Record (F2050) for all inmates involved in the incident.

Checklist 8 (Miscellaneous Documents) contains the Wing Record, the Gatekeeper's Daily Occurrence Book and Mercury Intelligence reports.

CHAPTER FOUR
THE DIFFERENT TYPES OF CLAIM

4.1 Introduction

Typically, in claims brought against prisons, the claim is made up of several different types of claim, for instance, negligence, trespass to the person (assault/battery), misfeasance in public office, or false imprisonment and breach of human rights. In this Chapter, we summarise how each of these types of claim work, and then we examine various cases where they were considered by the courts.

4.2 Vicarious liability

Vicarious liability is the doctrine that allows the court to hold an employer directly liable (without proof of fault) for the employee's actions or omissions. It is the way in which the prisoner essentially holds the Prison Service accountable for the wrongs of their employees, or in a private prison, the private company itself.

4.3 Negligence

The claim commonly made here is that a prison had a duty to protect a prisoner from some harm. That harm might be an accident on prison premises, a failure to give them the correct medical treatment or a failure to protect them from assaults by other prisoners.

As we will see in Chapter Five, the duty of care may be framed as a direct duty that falls on the Prison Service, or a duty that falls on one of its employees, for which the Prison Service is vicariously liable. Alternatively, it might be a non-delegable duty of care, in other words a duty for which the Prison Service cannot escape liability even though it carries out the duty through a separate organisation such as a private healthcare provider.

Generally speaking, the court will find that there is a common law duty of care on the part of the Prison Service to protect prisoners from harm. However, as we will see in Chapter Five on Caselaw below, that duty can be restricted. Alternatively, the negligence might relate to a failure to calculate a prisoner's release correctly and let the prisoner out, but failed to do so. That negligence could result in a psychiatric injury, from stress caused by unlawful imprisonment.

4.4 Trespass to the person, *Wilkinson v Downton*, the Protection from Harassment Act 1997 and the Equality Act 2010

Physical or emotional attacks on a prisoner come under the tort of trespass to the person. There are three main types of trespass to the person :-

- Battery – the actual infliction of unlawful force on another person.
- Assault – an act that causes another person to apprehend the infliction of immediate, unlawful force on his person, which could include threats of violence. So, it can be committed by threatening words alone.
- False imprisonment – with which we deal below.

In case law, the media and in this book, the word "battery" is rarely found, and is covered by the term "assault".

Assault and false imprisonment claims can be brought without any proof of damage, although obviously there needs to be an enquiry as to precisely what damage or injury has been sustained.

Generally speaking, the courts will find the Prison Service vicariously liable for batteries or assaults committed by prison officers. However, prison officers are of course allowed to use force, for instance to restrain prisoners, and frequently that will be their defence.

The tort of trespass to the person requires the intentional and direct infliction of harm. In ***Wilkinson v Downton [1897] 2 QB 57*** the court held that the Claimant could sue for the untoward consequences of a practical joke. In the actual case, the practical joke caused the Claimant, who was found to be a person of normal fortitude, to suffer a violent psychiatric reaction.

Section 1 of the Protection from Harassment Act 1997 makes it a criminal offence to pursue a course of conduct which the Defendant knows amounts to harassment of another person. Section 3 makes this offence actionable in a civil court.

Section 119 of the Equality Act 2010 permits a county court to grant a remedy where there has been a contravention of a provision referred to in Section 114(1) of the Act, which is briefly discrimination in relation to a protected characteristic, which is age, disability, gender reassignment, marriage and civil partnership, pregnancy and maternity, race, religion or belief, sex and sexual orientation. Section 26 of the Act prohibit harassment and Section 27 victimisation, both of which terms are closely defined.

There is a tight limitation period of six months under Section 118 of the 2010 Act which can be extended by such period as the court thinks just and equitable.

4.5 Misfeasance in public office

Misfeasance in public office can occur where prison officers or some other kind of detention official intentionally or recklessly sets out to cause the prisoner injury or keep him detained, despite the fact there is no legal basis for doing so. In contrast to trespass to the person claims, there must be some loss or damage for a claim for misfeasance to be brought. In the case of ***Karagozlu v Commissioner of the Police for the Metropolis [2006] EWCA Civ 1691*** the Court of Appeal decided that loss of liberty is a form of special or material damage sufficient to support a claim for misfeasance in public office if the other ingredients of the tort are made out.

It is a very difficult tort to prove, but there are examples (particularly in the Prison Service) of officers abusing their power.

The tort has a particular advantage over the tort of negligence. It may be that a court refuses to find for a Claimant in a negligence claim because there is no duty of care in that situation. One example outside the Prison Service might be a claim against the police for allowing a murderer to remain at large. A misfeasance in public office claim might succeed where it could be proved that the police had some corrupt purpose for acting in that way.

In the case of ***Three Rivers DC v Bank of England (No 3) [2003] 2 AC 1*** Lord Steyn in the House of Lords set out the two forms of the tort of misfeasance in public office :-

- Targeted malice by a public officer, i.e. conduct specifically intended to injure a person or persons. This type of case involves bad faith in the sense of the exercise of public power for an improper or ulterior motive.

- Where a public officer acts knowing he has no power to do the act complained of and that the act will probably injure the Claimant.

In ***London Borough of Southwark v Dennett [2007] EWCA Civ 1091*** Lord Justice May considered the state of knowledge that a Claimant must prove a defendant to have had as regards the second form of the tort, untargeted malice. Mere reckless indifference without the addition of subjective recklessness will not do. The Claimant must identify those said to have acted with subjective recklessness.

4.6 False imprisonment or wrongful detention

Prisoners and detainees often find themselves detained in circumstances where their imprisonment is unlawful. This may be for a number of reasons, for instance, unjustified behaviour by prison officers, wrongful exercise of the power to detain or an administrative error in the calculation of the period for which a prisoner can be detained. As we will see in Chapter Five on Caselaw, it is also possible for a prisoner to be wrongfully detained whilst serving their sentence in prison.

The tort of false imprisonment has two ingredients: the fact of imprisonment and the absence of lawful authority to justify it.

In cases of administrative error, the way in which the courts actually determine whether any these claims are successful, is quite complex and requires a detailed understanding of sentencing law and guidelines. It also requires an understanding of the caselaw, and we examine several cases in Chapter Five.

4.7 Human Rights claims

The Human Rights Act 1998 which came into force on the 1st October 2000 incorporates into English law rights under the European Convention for the Protection of Human Rights and Fundamental Freedoms. Under Section 2 of the 1998 Act, the court has an obligation to interpret the UK law in a way that is compatible with the Convention right.

The focus of the European Convention is the protection of human rights, not the award of compensation (although that most certainly remains a remedy). The intention of the 1998 Act is to ensure that domestic legislation is compatible with human rights legislation. If it is not then there may be a remedy.

Section 7 of the Act provides that a person who claims that a public authority has acted (or proposes to act) in a way made unlawful by Section 6(1) has two separate remedies:

- He can bring proceedings against the authority pursuant to the 1998 Act, i.e. effectively an action for breach of statutory duty in the sense of a violation of a Convention right.
- He can rely on the Convention right either in a claim brought on a conventional basis or as a defence or issue in proceedings brought against him by a public authority.

A court can award damages for a human rights breach under Section 8 of the 1998 Act, although it is not obliged to and sometimes, it will simply award costs. The European Court of Human Rights has said that there must be a clear causal connection between the damage claims by the Claimant and the violation of the Convention right. Section 8(4) says that in awarding damages the court must take into account the principles applied by the European Court of Human Rights,,who apply the principle of "just satisfaction" under Article 41 of the Convention.

The amounts awarded by the European Court of Human Rights and our UK courts for breach of human rights are generally very much lower than the amounts awarded in under domestic tortious claims.

In ***R (Greenfield) v Secretary of State for the Home Department [2005] UKHL 14*** a prison governor conducted the hearing of a disciplinary charge against a prisoner, found him guilty and ordered the prisoner to serve 21 additional days of imprisonment. The prisoner brought a claim to contend that the hearing before the governor infringed his right under Article 6 of the European Convention on Human Rights to a fair hearing before an independent tribunal in respect of a criminal charge. The prisoner claimed damages for violation of Article 6. The House of Lords found that there had been a breach of Article 6 as alleged, but held that the finding of violation was sufficient 'just satisfaction' and that no substantive damages equivalent to damages for false imprisonment should be awarded. The House of Lords rejected the submission of the prisoner that damages should be awarded as just satisfaction under section 8 of the HRA assessed by reference to levels of damages for false imprisonment in domestic law. In ***Michael v Chief Constable of South Wales [2015] UKSC 2*** the UK Supreme Court said that whereas civil actions were designed to compensate for losses, human rights claims were intended to uphold minimum rights. Consequently, the approach to damages should be different.

However more recently, the first instance judgment of Mr Justice Leggatt in ***Alseran and Others v the Ministry of Defence [2017] EWHC 3289 (QB)*** which involved the mistreatment of Iraqi nationals by British soldiers, deals with the case of overlapping tortious and human rights claims. That judgment suggests that where a victim is being compensated for human rights, he should receive similar compensation for the harm suffered to that which would be awarded on a parallel claim in tort.

The main Articles used in a claim by a prisoner are :-

- Article 2 – protection of life
- Article 3 – protection against torture or inhuman or degrading treatment or punishment
- Article 5 – protection against arbitrary detention
- Article 8 – protection for private and family life
- Article 14 – protection against discrimination

Human rights claims have a very tight limitation, which is under Section 7(5)(a) of the 1998 Act one year "*beginning with the date on which the act complained of took place.*" Section 7(5)(b) provides the court with discretion to override the time period, however that Section makes no mention of the fact that the Claimant might be a child or lacking mental capacity, which would override or extend limitation under the Limitation Act 1980. Although there is some case law where courts have used their discretion under Section 7(5)(b), practitioners are strongly advised to initiate proceedings before the one-year time limit, or seek a limitation moratorium from the Defendant.

CHAPTER FIVE
CASELAW

5.1 Introduction

In this Chapter, we examine various judgments from the courts that deal with specific issues that come up in personal injury claims. There is a considerable of overlap between those issues, because so often, a series of different claims are being brought. We begin with injuries from assaults that could have been prevented by the Prison Service and move on to failure to prevent psychiatric damage. Some caution needs to be exercised with the earlier cases, given that prison procedures and practices have changed markedly over the years, and the courts may expect higher standards of prison officers.

We then look at how the doctrine of vicarious liability in ***Cox v Ministry of Justice [2014] EWCA Civ 132*** and the Occupiers' Liability Act 1957 helped the Claimants in their cases. After that we come to the two judgment of ***GB v Home Office [2015] EWHC 819 (QB) 1*** and more recently, ***Razumas v Ministry of Justice [2018] EWHC 215 (QB)*** which examine the issue of negligent healthcare in prisons, where the actual healthcare was provided by a private contractor.

GB and ***Razumas*** demonstrate the difficulty that arises for Claimants when health care functions of the Prison Service are contracted out to private organisations, or simply made the responsibility of the NHS. In ***GB***, it was held that the Home Office could owe a non-delegable duty in relation to healthcare services provided to inmates, but in ***Razumas***, the court decided that although there was a limited direct duty in relation to medical care, there was no non-delegable duty. The deciding factor appears to have the complex legislation behind the re-allocation of healthcare responsibilities. For this reason, the selection of the correct Defendant at an early stage in the case is crucial. These cases do at least show the way in which a court will decide on a Defendant' liability by reference to the statutory framework.

We also look at wrongful detention cases. These cases work on a different basis to the assault and negligence based claims that we mentioned above. The crucial question for the court will be whether the detention was lawful. Sometimes the unlawful nature of a detention comes from absence of any right to detain, and sometimes from a simple miscalculation of the prisoner's sentence.

Finally, we look at claims based on human rights.

5.2 Failure to protect a prisoner from assaults by other prisoners

These claims can be, in practice, very difficult to bring. This is because courts accept that prisoners cannot be constantly segregated or supervised, and the sudden and seemingly unprovoked nature of these assaults makes them very difficult to predict or prevent. Nonetheless there are a number of cases where prisoner have succeeded in showing that the system failed to protect them. Sometimes the mistake made can be something quite simple, such as a failure to place a prison officer in a particular place as happened in ***Hartshorn v Home Office [1999] CLY 4012, 21 July 1999 (CA).***

Palmer v Home Office, the Guardian, 31 March 1988, CA

The Claimant was stabbed with a pair of scissors by a fellow prisoner in the prison's tailor's workshop. The assailant had been convicted of three murders as well as other very serious offences of violence. He was described as a vicious, dangerous and psychopathic murderer. His conduct in prison included an assault on a prison officer and the governor had information that he had acquired a razor blade, which he intended to use on prison officers and the public and that he intended to kill the governor. He was said to be a cold, angry, bitter man but on the other hand, he was also said to be the best cleaner that the tailor's shop had had. The day before the attack the assistant governor received a report that three hacksaw blades were found on the assailant. Certain privileges were taken away from him but he was permitted to continue working in the tailor's workshop.

The Claimant's case was dismissed at first instance and the matter came before the Court of Appeal. In his judgment, Lord Justice Neill said that those in charge of prisons had a difficult task. Except in extreme cases they could not keep prisoners permanently locked up or segregated. It was necessary, wherever possible to provide them with employment. The assistant governor's assessment was that the assailant, though dangerous, was not a particular risk. It was quite impossible to say that the decision taken by the assistant governor the day before the attack was negligent. Consequently, it was not negligent to employ him in the workshop.

Neill LJ quoted with approval a passage in Halsbury's Laws, 4th Edition, Vol 37, para 1140, which was to the following effect:

"The duty on those responsible for one of Her Majesty's prisons is to take reasonable care for the safety of those who are within, including the prisoners. Actions will lie, for example, where a prisoner sustains injury at the hands of another prisoner in consequence of the negligent supervision of the prison authorities, with greater care and attention, to the extent that it is reasonable and practicable, being required of a prisoner known to be potentially at greater risk than other prisoners; or if negligently put to work in conditions damaging to health; or if inadequately instructed in the use of machinery; or if injured as a result of defective premises."

Hartshorn v Home Office [1999] CLY 4012, 21 July 1999 (CA)

The Claimant was a prisoner serving a life sentence. He was slashed across the face by two other prisoners, who used a razor blade. The assault occurred at a time when tea was being served on the wing which the Claimant occupied and when prisoners from other wings were allowed to associate with one another. The assailants (who came from another wing to the Claimant) were on the ground floor hall of the prison and the Claimant was on one of the upper floors. Prisoners on the ground floor were forbidden from going up the stairs to the upper floors. There were no prison officers on the upper floors, and the prison officer on the ground floor hall had gone away briefly on an errand. There was no reason for the prison to suspect that there was a grudge between the assailants and the Claimant. The assailants went up the stairs and called to the Claimant to come down at which point, they slashed him across the face with a razor.

The trial judge allowed the claim. He found that the Home Office was in breach of its duty by failing to station a prison officer at the foot of the stairs and that had that been done, the assault would have been prevented. The Home Office appealed.

The Court of Appeal dismissed the Home Office's appeal. Although the risk of assault from other prisoners was not a serious one and it was impossible to segregate prisoners or supervise them all the time, it was recognized nonetheless as a risk and the rule prohibiting prisoners from going upstairs was designed to give some protection and in part designed to stop prisoners attacking one another. The Home Office should have taken reasonable care to ensure that this rule was obeyed by having an officer present in the area. Ordinarily the prison officer on duty on the ground floor would have been present, and it was only by chance that he was absent. Had he been present, the assault would on the balance of probabilities not have occurred.

Thompson v Home Office [2001] EWCA Civ 331

The Claimant was a prisoner in a Young Offender Institution, Swinfen Hall. He was attacked in the association area of the prison by another prisoner who slashed his face with a razor blade. He brought a claim against the Home Officer for failing to prevent the attack. He did not give evidence to say who his attacker was offer any positive evidence of the nature of the weapon used. At trial however, the judge found that it was an unprovoked attack by another inmate using a razor blade and that finding was not challenged by the Home Office. The claim proceeded on the basis that the system at Swinfen Hall for providing and recovering razor blades was negligent.

The Home Office did not dispute that they owed the Claimant a duty to take reasonable care for his safety, but they denied that they were in breach of that duty. They had followed Home Office guidelines about razors and their system was such that, balancing all relevant considerations, they discharged their duty of care. Alternatively, the Home Office said that the Claimant's unfortunate injuries were not caused by any breach of duty on their part.

At first instance, the Claimant succeeded and the case came before the Court of Appeal. Lord Justice May (with whom the remainder of the court agreed) allowed the appeal. He considered all of the evidence that had been put in front of the trial judge. His conclusion was that prison governors, and especially those in charge of Young Offender Institutions, had to make balancing judgments between tight security and a regime aimed at rehabilitation in which the inmates were required to exercise responsibility. The principal security officer at Swinfen Hall had said in evidence that instituting a system of withdrawing razors from prisoners each day would provide a greater degree of control, but that it would be at a cost to something else in the regime. A balance had to be maintained. If there was a problem with razor attacks, the principal security officer would advocate doing something about it, but in his view, Swinfen Hall did not have a problem. Razor blade weapons were not common at all.

The Claimant's evidence did not establish that the basic system for razors in operation at Swinfen Hall was negligently adopted. The adoption of the basic system was a considered decision in the exercise of a balancing discretion and the fact that a more restrictive system operated in other institutions did not establish that the system in operation in Swinfen Hall was negligent. A regime for razors could not be judged by reference to the system for missing tools in the workshop for which substantially different considerations applied. There was no proper basis for rejecting the prison officers' evidence that razor attacks at Swinfen Hall were uncommon and essentially not a problem. The Claimant had said in his oral evidence that there had been 10 attacks in two years, but the trial judge rightly observed that this was gossip and it did not accord with the records. Further the restrictive system operated at some other institutions was not a complete answer to the problem of missing razors and it was unrealistic to focus on razor blades as if their elimination would by itself remove all similar risk, particularly as prisoners used other types of offensive implement.

Stenning v Home Office [2002] EWCA Civ 793

The Claimant was a prisoner serving a life sentence for serious sexual offences. On the 27th December 1996, he was held hostage by another prisoner in a cell for about five hours. When prison officers eventually stormed the cell, the Claimant suffered serious stab wounds and subsequently he suffered post-traumatic stress disorder. The initial imprisonment by the fellow prisoner occurred at a time when prisoners on the wing were allowed to leave their cells to watch videos, play games, go to the canteen or generally have freedom from the confines of their cells. The assailant was a Category A prisoner. He had been sentenced to life imprisonment for attempting to murder a woman. He was a man of low intelligence, and he suffered from a personality disorder which made him behave in a childish way. In 1987-8, when he was diagnosed as having clear psychopathic characteristics, he spent six months at the secure hospital at Rampton. Because of his behaviour, he was disciplined on over 50 different occasions during the course of his prison career. He was also moved from time to time within the secure prison estate, in order to relieve the staff in any particular prison from the burden of managing him for too long a period. At the time of the incident, there was no evidence that he was having treatment for any identifiable mental disorder susceptible to treatment at the time. Prior to December 1985, he had threatened other prisoners and prison officers, but since that time there had been no acts of violence of the same degree of seriousness. He arrived at Wakefield Prison in 1995 and there was evidence that he told a psychologist in February 1996 that he felt like killing an inmate to secure a move from Wakefield, and that he wrote to the governor along these lines two months later. He was well known on his prison wing for being constantly abusive and threatening but it appeared that prison officers were managing his behaviour.

On the 23rd September 1996, the assailant's wing governor wrote a letter to the Prison Service headquarters, which was responsible for managing prisoners with life sentences. The assailant had been agitating to move prisons, and the governor in his letter said that although the assailant was being managed by his staff, "*I fear that should we fail to move him he may do something in an effort to force our hand.*" This letter was written after the governor had heard the assailant threaten to kill a sex offender if he was not moved.

The trial judge found for the Claimant but the decision was reversed by the Court of Appeal. Whilst expressing sympathy for the Claimant the court said that the letter of the 23rd September 1996 had to be seen in the context of all the other evidence that was available. There were a number of other prisoners who were equally demanding and would also offer all sorts of threats to try and ensure they were moved to another prison. The assailant was being managed and prison officers believed that he was making progress.

The Court of Appeal said that a judgment had been made, by experienced prison officers, that it would be better to keep the assailant for the time being in the one prison where he had been able to live a relatively managed existence. There was no evidence at all that anyone thought he posed an immediate threat to a fellow inmate. Whilst there might be cases where a judge could properly make a finding that experienced prison officers were negligent in carrying out a risk assessment because the evidence overwhelmingly called for action on their part which they did not take, this was not such a case. It would have been quite wrong for any judge to make a finding of negligence in this case without the help of a witness expert in the difficult discipline of risk assessment.

Stenning should be compared with the findings of the Court of Appeal in an earlier case – ***Gill v Home Office Unreported Court of Appeal 6th July 2000.*** The full transcript can be found on Westlaw at *[2000] 7 WLUK 109*. The Home Office was held liable in negligence for an assault upon the Claimant, a prison officer by another prisoner, who had been at the prison for only a matter of hours before the assault occurred. The prisoner was regarded as psychologically disturbed and a threat to both officers and other prisoners. He had been assessed by prison staff on arrival. The trial judge found that there was a foreseeable risk of injury to prison officers, because of the ample evidence of the danger presented by the prisoner. The sensible course would have been, to keep him under observation and to apply routine security measures. This meant keeping him in his cell, but he was let out temporarily by another prison officer, The Court of Appeal agreed with that assessment.

5.3 Failure to prevent psychiatric harm

Home Office v Butchart [2006] EWCA Civ 239

The Claimant was a prisoner who was assessed as being at risk of self harm. In accordance with Prison Service policy he was placed in a shared cell, but his cellmate was seriously mentally and killed himself. He was then moved to another cell with a prisoner who was also at risk of suicide. He claimed damages for being placed with the prisoner who took his life, for being blamed for that suicide and then being placed with another suicidal prisoner.

The Home Office tried to strike out the claim on the basis that they owed the Claimant no duty of care to prevent his psychiatric injury as a result of his cellmate's suicide, and in any event his injury was not foreseeable. The essence of the Home Office's case was based on the judgment in ***Frost v Chief Constable of South Yorkshire Police [1999] 2 AC 455***. This case set out the "control mechanisms" that limit the right of a person to make a personal injury claim, when they are a mere bystander. These control mechanisms included as a necessary element the fact that the Claimant must have close ties of love and affection with the victim, which plainly in this case he did not.

At first instance the judge refused to strike out the claim, and the Home Office's appeal to the Court of Appeal was dismissed. Lord Justice Latham said in the Court of Appeal that the case of ***Frost*** did not apply here. The Claimant's case was not one simply based on the effect of his cell mate's suicide. It was not a "nervous shock" case. The psychiatric injury that he ultimately suffered was the result of a breach of a primary duty of care owed to him. It was the result of the cumulative effect of being incarcerated with an increasingly disturbed man, who committed suicide in circumstances which gave rise to a feeling of guilt on the part of the Claimant which was compounded by the remark of the prison officer apparently ascribing responsibility to him, and a further period, albeit short, of incarceration with yet another prisoner suffering from suicidal thoughts.

The real question was whether or not the relationship between the Claimant and the Home Office gave rise to a duty of care which encompassed a duty to take reasonable steps to avoid psychiatric harm. In the present case there is no doubt that the Home Office owed a duty of care to those in its custody. In the view of the Court of Appeal, the pleaded facts were sufficient to establish, if proved, that the appellant knew or ought to have known that the respondent was a prisoner vulnerable to psychiatric harm. In those circumstances it was inevitable that the duty of care which the Home Office owned to the Claimant included a duty to take reasonable steps to minimise the risk of psychiatric harm. Clearly the assessment of what steps could or should have been taken would be a matter of debate on an assessment of the evidence, bearing in mind the fact that the Claimant was a prisoner and that the Home Office's responsibilities had to be assessed in the light of the inevitable constraints imposed by what was reasonably practicable in a prison community.

Burn v Ministry of Justice [2012] EWHC 876

A prisoner described by the court as "violent, devious and cunning" was held at HMP Wormwood Scrubs. On the 8th January 2007 he feigned illness in his cell and persuaded a prison doctor that he was having or had had an epileptic fit. He was then taken to Hammersmith Hospital chained to a gurney and handcuffed to one of the three prison officers. On arrival the ambulance doors were opened by two friends of the prisoner. One had a handgun, the other brandished a large pair of bolt croppers and both wore masks. They threatened the prison officers, who complying with their training, released the prisoner. Each of the Claimants suffered psychiatric injury in the form of PTSD. They alleged that this was caused by a breach of duty on the part of the Prison Service.

Mr Justice Mackay said that all the witnesses had given evidence to the effect that whatever the views of the security people in a prison the decision to transfer a prisoner out of the prison to a hospital was a medical one to be taken by a prison doctor. It could not be overridden. Expert evidence had been given as to whether the doctor was right to make that decision. Mackay J said that the doctor on the day of the incident, was in a very difficult position. He had observed this patient and had also plainly made some enquiries of the wing staff about this man. He could have obtained rectal diazepam and administered it, but that would have very difficult. Alternatively, he could have told the staff to lock the prisoner in his cell and to leave him as he was. In the judgment of Mackay J, faced with those choices he could not accept that the decision taken by the doctor was one which no reasonably competent prison doctor in his circumstances would have taken. The claim must fail.

The earlier unreported case of ***Armstrong v Home Office Unreported Mr Justice Owen 8th October 2001*** concerns a claim brought by a prison officer for psychiatric injury sustained whilst handling Rosemary West, the wife of the serial killer, Fred West. Her case was that she was exposed to a reasonably foreseeable risk of psychiatric injury by virtue of the time that she was required to spend with West and because she was actively encouraged to establish a close relationship with West so as to prevent her from committing suicide. Ultimately her claim was dismissed. A full report of the judgment can be found on Westlaw at *[2001] 10 WLUK 177.*

5.4 Duty to pass on information and specific defences to a claim based on failure to prevent suicide

In ***Kirkham v. Chief Constable of the Greater Manchester Police [1989] Civ 3*** the police failed to fill out a form properly, warning the prison authorities that the prison in question was at risk of committing suicide, and whilst in a remand centre, he took his life. The police argued that they owed the deceased prisoner no duty of care to pass on the information in their possession. The Court of Appeal held that the police authorities had a duty to pass on information about the suicidal tendencies of a detainee to the prison authorities. As a matter of principle, when one person was in the lawful custody of another, there was a duty upon the person having custody of another to take all reasonable steps to avoid acts or omissions which he could reasonably foresee would be likely to harm the person for whom he was responsible.

The Court of Appeal said that it had no difficulty in holding that the police assumed certain responsibilities towards the prisoner when they took him into custody, and in particular assumed a responsibility to pass on information which might affect his well-being when he was transferred from their custody to the custody of the prison authorities.

The police in this case raised another defence. They said that they were not liable to pay the prisoner's widow because he had inflicted the injury on himself deliberately. This is the defence otherwise known as "*volenti non fit injuria*". The Court of Appeal rejected this argument. Whilst the deceased was sane in the legal sense, when he took his life, his suicide was a deliberate and conscious act. However, he was suffering from clinical depression and his judgment was impaired. Finally, the police also relied on the defence that the deceased prisoner had, by taking his own life, committed the "wrong" himself. They relied on the doctrine "*ex turpi causa non oritur action*".

Again, the Court of Appeal rejected this argument. Suicide was no longer a crime following the Suicide Act 1961 which indicate a change in attitudes and there was previous caselaw showing that remedies had been granted for failure to prevent suicide.

In ***Reeves -v- The Commissioner of Police of the Metropolis [1999] UKHL 35*** the deceased was known to be a suicide risk. He had been brought to a police station having tried to kill himself in a cell at the Magistrates' court. He was examined by a doctor, who, whilst concluding that he was not suffering from any mental illness or other mental disturbance, considered him to be a suicide risk and left instructions that he should be observed frequently. Within 25 minutes of his being returned to his cell after being examined by the doctor, he had managed to hang himself from material from his shirt which he had secured through the open spy-hole to the cell. The trial judge concluded that the police had been negligent. He held, however, that the deceased had been of sound mind, and that in those circumstances, his suicide was a *novus actus interveniens*, and he dismissed the action. He expressed the view that if he had considered that that defence was not available he would have held the deceased 100% to blame, and accordingly awarded no damages in any event.

The Court of Appeal by a majority, allowed the appeal on the grounds that the suicide, being the very act against which the police had been required to guard, did not constitute a *novus actus interveniens*, but that damages fell to be reduced as a result of the deceased's "fault" under the Law Reform (Contributory Negligence) Act 1945. However, that responsibility should be assessed at 0%.

The House of Lords came to a different conclusion. Although they agreed that the defence of *novus actus interveniens* did not apply, they would not (by a majority) impose a 100% apportionment of responsibility to the deceased prisoner under the 1945 Act. To do so would simply be a different way of saying that the police should not have owed the deceased a duty of care. However, they would substitute a finding of 50% apportionment.

5.5 Vicarious liability for negligence – *Cox v Ministry of Justice [2014] EWCA Civ 132*

On the 10th September 2007, while working as the catering manager at HM Prison Swansea, the Claimant was injured in an accident caused by the negligence of a prisoner carrying out paid work under her supervision. The Claimant had four members of staff under her in the staff hierarchy, three civilians and one prison officer. Two of these subordinates would be on duty at any one time. Approximately, twenty prisoners would be assigned each day to kitchen work. Such prisoners would sometimes be regularly engaged in this work. Others would assist over short periods. On the day in question, at about 9.15 a.m., a delivery of supplies for the kitchen arrived on the ground floor. The Claimant went to attend to the delivery, taking with her six prisoners who were to bring the delivered food supplies from the ground floor to the first floor. Due to the breakdown of the lift, the prisoners were instructed by the Claimant to carry the loads manually. One of the prisoners dropped one of the sacks which burst open, spilling rice onto the floor. The Claimant instructed all the prisoners to stop work until the spillage was cleared. She then dispatched one prisoner to fetch the necessary cleaning equipment and bent down on one knee to prop up the damaged sack, in order to prevent further spillage. As she straightened up to stand, she felt a heavy thud on her upper back. Another prisoner had ignored the Claimant's instruction to stop work and had attempted to carry two sacks past the kneeling Claimant. However, he lost his balance and hit his head on an adjacent wall. One of the sacks which he was carrying fell off his shoulder and onto the Claimant's back.

The claim against the Defendant was made on three bases. First, it was argued that the Defendant was vicariously liable for the negligence of the prisoner who dropped the sack on the Claimant. Secondly, it was said that the Defendant was in breach of its personal duty to the Claimant as her employer to take reasonable care for her safety by providing a safe system of work, a safe place of work and safe staff and equipment. Thirdly, the contention was that the Defendant was in breach of its statutory duty under Regulation 5(1) of the Workplace (Health, Safety and Welfare) Regulations 1992 and under Regulation 5(1) of the Provision and Use of Work Equipment Regulations 1998 (in each case in failing to keep the lift in proper repair).

The trial judge dismissed the claims under all these heads. In relation to the first claim, he said that the Defendant was not vicariously liable for the negligent actions of the prisoner. The Claimant submitted that he was wrong to do so in respect of the first two heads. The third head of claim, based on the two sets of Regulations, was no longer pursued.

The case came before the Court of Appeal. Lord Justice McCombe said that the negligent prisoner received pay, at the rate of £11.55 per week, for the kitchen work on which he was engaged at the time of the accident. The prisoner's pay was received under the Prison Rules 1999 and in accordance with the policy to be found in the Prison Service Order PSO 4460. There was also a "domestic" document produced at Swansea Prison regulating prisoners' work and a Kitchen Induction document.

McCombe LJ considered the law on vicarious liability. In the case of *Various Claimants v Catholic Child Welfare Society [2012] UKSC* 56 Lord Phillips identified four particular areas of development:

- It was now possible for an unincorporated association to be liable for the tortious acts of one or more of its members.

- A defendant might also be liable for the act of a tortfeasor even though the act in question involved a violation of a duty owed by the tortfeasor to the defendant and even if the act in question was a criminal offence.

- Vicarious liability could even extend to liability for a criminal act of sexual assault.

- It was also possible for two different defendants to be vicariously liable for the single tortious act of a tortfeasor.

There were differences from the normal employment relationship insofar as (i) the prisoners were bound to the Defendant not by contract, but by their sentences of imprisonment, (ii) while the prisoners were paid, the wages were nominal. However, these differences from the normal employment relationship rendered the relationship between the prisoners and Defendant, in the conduct of this activity, if anything closer than that of an employer and its employees. McCombe LJ would hold that the Defendant was vicariously liable for the injury caused to the Claimant and would allow the appeal on that basis.

In relation to direct liability, this did not need to be addressed, but McCombe LJ expressed his opinion on the issue. The judge had made findings as to the likely content of training and as to what might have happened if training had been provided. These were unassailable findings of fact on both duty and causation with which the Court of Appeal should not interfere. The fact remained that the risk was obvious. The prisoner chose to ignore both the obvious risk and the express instruction of the Claimant. The trial judge was, therefore, entitled to conclude that no training would have caused him to do otherwise. Therefore, the appeal would not have been allowed on this ground, but it would be allowed on the issue of vicarious liability.

5.6 G4S Care and Justice Services (UK) Ltd v Manley [2016] EWHC 2355 (QB) – Occupiers' Liability Act 1957

There was an electrical failure in a prison, which caused the cell light to go out. The Claimant had previously undergone a hip operation which mean that he could only walk with the aid of crutches and he had a weak leg. When the light went off he reported it to a prison officer, who then reported it to a senior prison officer who eventually restored the power. The prisoner needed to use the toilet, but as it was dark, he fell and suffered injury. The judge found that as a fact that it should have taken 10 or 15 minutes, or at most 20 minutes, to restore the power depending on where the senior officer was in the prison and whether he was immediately contactable. The failure to restore electricity within a reasonable time in the circumstances of this case amounted to a breach of the duty under section 2(2) of the Occupiers' Liability Act 1957, which was to take reasonable care to ensure that the Claimant was reasonably safe in using certain premises. The Defendant appealed on the grounds that that the judge erred by not asking the correct question, namely whether the premises were, as an objective fact, unsafe. Secondly, the Defendant contended that the judge had placed an unreasonably high standard of care on the Defendant.

The appeal came before Mr Justice Lewis in the High Court. In relation to the first issue, the duty of care recognised by section 2(2) of the 1957

Act was a duty "*to take such care as in all the circumstances is reasonable to see that the visitor will be reasonably safe in using the premises for the purposes for which he is invited or permitted*" to be there. Previous caselaw had established that the trial judge had to address his mind to the question of whether premises were, in fact unsafe. Lewis J said that the judge had referred to Section 2 and the test that it set out. The senior prison officer was told about the power failure but he was not told, and should have been told, that the Claimant who had reported the power failure was concerned that he had reduced mobility and was less able to look after himself when the lighting conditions in his cell were as poor as they were. The urgency should have been communicated to the senior officer and had it been the senior officer would have been rectified the problem within a reasonable time which could have been as little as ten minutes. Furthermore, that was in a context where the reasonable time for dealing with power failure was 15 to 20 minutes and the officer took far longer to restore power in the present case. In the circumstances, therefore, the judge applied the right test.

In relation to the second issue, this was not a case of the judge simply treating a delay of 15 to 20 minutes beyond a target time as involving a breach of the duty in Section 2 of the 1957 Act. The essential findings, were that the officer was told that the power was out in the cell and that there was a degree of urgency as the Claimant had recently come out of hospital and had mobility problems but the officer failed to pass that information on. Nothing said by the judge in this particular judgment required the Defendant to carry out a risk assessment of the precise medical condition of all prisoners and then to tailor responses to power failures according to a scale of vulnerability to falling in unusually dark conditions. The appeal by the Defendant would be dismissed.

5.7 *St George v Home Office [2008] EWCA Civ 1068 – contributory negligence*

The Claimant, a serving prisoner fell from his bunk bed following a seizure caused by withdrawal from alcohol and drugs. The trial judge found that the Home Office were in breach of duty in (i) allocating the claimant to a top bunk when, to the knowledge of prison staff, he had a history of substance abuse and withdrawal seizure while in prison; (ii) not protecting his airway from obstruction between the time of his fall and the arrival of the ambulance crew and not administering oxygen to him during that time; and (iii) being responsible for various failures which combined to delay the claimant's arrival at hospital until 19.25 hours. The judge found, however, that this delay did not contribute to his brain damage. The judge also found that the Claimant was 15% to blame for the accident, and reduced his claim accordingly.

The Home Office appealed on a number of issues, and the judgment of the Court of Appeal is mainly about the issue of causation. In relation to contributory negligence this was appealed by the Claimant. The trial judge had found that the Claimant had to be described as being at fault in relation to the choices he had made in his life prior to the events of his accident. That fault had caused or contributed to the injuries not because they have put him in prison, but because he was knowingly risking injury to his health by doing what he was doing, even if he did not know how it would happen. On the other hand, the Prison Service failed in its duty to him by some clear margin and the prison service should have been better prepared to deal with epileptic emergencies than it was at least on that occasion. They should clearly shoulder the majority of responsibility for this event.

The Court of Appeal held that the judge was entitled to hold that the Claimant was at fault in becoming addicted to drugs and alcohol when he was 15 or 16 years of age. He was also entitled to infer that the claimant must have known at that time that the abuse of drugs and alcohol on the scale necessary to lead to addiction was dangerous to his health. Finally, he was entitled to conclude, without the benefit of medical evidence, that the Home Office had discharged the burden of proving fault.

However the Claimant was not injured "as a result partly of his own fault" within the meaning of section 1(1) of the Law Reform (Contributory Negligence) Act 1945 because his injuries were not caused partly by his addiction which was the result of his lifestyle decisions. The fault was not sufficiently closely connected with the Defendant's negligence. Rather it was part of the Claimant's history which had led to his being a man who was suffering from a particular medical condition. Consequently, the damages should not have been reduced.

5.8 Negligent healthcare in an immigration removal centre

In *GB v Home Office [2015] EWHC 819 (QB) 1* the Claimant was a Nigerian national who was detained at Yarl's Wood detention centre as an illegal over-stayer in the United Kingdom. On her arrival on the 19th June 2012 she had a medical screening and then on the 21st June 2012 she was seen by a GP employed by a local GP surgery. He conducted an assessment and prescribed the Claimant with Mefloquine, an anti-malarial drug. This was because the Home Office, the Defendant was proposing to send the Claimant back to Nigeria and there were clear rules relating to the prescription of anti-malarial drugs to those who might be sent back to countries where malaria is commonplace. On the 10th July 2012, the Claimant was refused asylum and the decision was taken to remove her from the United Kingdom. However, it was the Claimant's case that from about that time onwards, she began to exhibit signs of psychosis. On the 16th July 2012, following an assessment by a consultant psychiatrist, it was suggested that the Claimant had a drug-induced psychosis, triggered by the Mefloquine, and that she was sectionable under the Mental Health Act 1983. On the 27th July 2012, she was released from detention and granted refugee status.

She pursued a claim for wrongful detention against the Defendant. However, this judgment related to her claim in negligence against the Defendant arising out of the medical treatment which she received whilst detained at Yarl's Wood. A hearing was ordered in relation to a preliminary issue as to two questions – namely :-

- Whether or not the Defendant owed a non-delegable duty of care to the Claimant so as to render it liable to the Claimant in respect of any negligence acts or omissions on the part of those providing medical care at Yarl's Wood (were such negligence to be established);

The issue of non-delegable duty had been examined in the UK Supreme Court judge in ***Woodland v Swimming Teachers Association and Others [2013] UKSC 66.***

- Further alternatively, whether or not the Defendant was vicariously liable for the acts or omissions of the medical practitioner and other Yarl's Wood health care staff.

Mr Justice Coulson considered the relevant statutory framework and regulations in relation to the contracting out of detention services by the Home Office. The relevant statute was the Immigration and Asylum Act 1999, specifically Part VIII Section 153 of the 1999 Act provided for the creation of the Detention Centre Rules, which set out how Immigration Removal Centres were to be run. Rule 33 dealt with health care and the need to have a medical practitioner in every detention centre. Coulson J also made reference to Section 5 of the Immigration Directorate's Instructions headed "*Inoculations and Other Preventative Treatment (Prophylaxis) For Persons Being Removed from the United Kingdom*" which dealt with the issue of preventive treatment for malaria. There was also the contract between the Defendant and Serco, although the contract between Serco and the doctors had not been found by either of them.

Coulson J considered the judgment in the case of ***Woodland*** and what it had to say about the establishment of a non-delegable duty of care. He set out the necessary criteria.

- The Claimant was a patient or a child, or for some other reason was especially vulnerable or dependent on the protection of the Defendant against the risk of injury. Other examples were likely to be prisoners and residents in care homes.

- There was an antecedent relationship between the Claimant and the Defendant, independent of the negligent act or omission itself, (i) which placed the Claimant in the actual custody, charge or care of the Defendant, and (ii) from which it was possible to impute to the Defendant the assumption of a positive duty to protect the Claimant from harm, and not just a duty to refrain from conduct which would foreseeably damage the Claimant.

- The Claimant had no control over how the Defendant chose to perform those obligations, i.e. whether personally or through employees or through third parties.

- The Defendant had delegated to a third party some function which was an integral part of the positive duty which he had assumed towards the Claimant; and the third party was exercising, for the purpose of the function thus delegated to him, the Defendant's custody or care of the Claimant and the element of control that went with it.

- The third party had been negligent not in some collateral respect but in the performance of the very function assumed by the Defendant and delegated by the Defendant to him.

Coulson J said that all five criteria were present in this case. In relation to whether there had been negligence, that remained to be determined at a future trial.

However, there was another test. The court also had to determine whether it was fair, just and reasonable for a non-delegable duty to lie in this case. Coulson J said that it should not be for the Claimant in this case to have to try and work out which private contractor or individual doctor might be liable for which failure, and then litigate on the basis of that assessment. She was detained by the Defendant; she was in the Defendant's control and she was entitled to look to the Defendant for proper protection. Accordingly, the imposition of a non-delegable duty in this case was fair, just and reasonable.

Coulson J made reference to a previous case with very similar facts – ***Christina Morgan v Ministry of Justice and Another [2010] EWHC 2248 (QB)*** where the court had refused to impose a non-delegable duty of care. However, that judgment came some years before the decision in ***Woodland*** and in a later case ***Amadou Nyang v G4S Care and Justice Services Ltd and Others [2013] EWHC 3946 (QB)***, a concession had been made by G4S that they owed a non-delegable duty to provide care for the physical and mental health of detainees.

There was another issue as to whether the Defendant was exempt was liability under the Crown Proceedings Act 1947. In judgment of Coulson J, Section 2(1)(a) of the 1947 Act extended the Crown's liabilities to its servants or agents, including independent contractors as defined by Section.38. That was sufficient to catch not only the Defendant, but those engaged by the Defendant, which would include for this purpose, Serco and/or the doctor.

Consequently, the answer to the first question as to whether there was a non-delegable duty in this case was in the affirmative. In those circumstances the second question – as to whether there was vicarious liability did not require to be answered.

5.9 Negligent healthcare in a prison

Steele v the Home Office EWCA Civ 724

The Claimant was a lifer detained in high security prisons with Category A status. He had sustained damage to his teeth while playing rugby football. During the 1980s and 1990s, he underwent extensive restorative work. Since his incarceration, he needed a good deal of dental treatment. In early 1998, while detained in HMP Belmarsh, the respondent lost a filling from one of his teeth. He was in considerable pain. He requested a dental appointment but, before one was provided, he was moved to HMP Full Sutton. It was not until October 1998 that he finally saw a dentist. Thereafter he had further problems with his teeth and again there were further delays in getting him treatment, together with substandard treatment. This went on until 2006. The trial judge held the Home Office liable in respect of the pain suffered during that period. He assessed damages for pain and suffering at £45,000. He also awarded £16,000 as future pecuniary loss, representing the cost of dental treatment which the respondent ought to have received on the NHS but had not received.

The Home Office partly appealed the decision of the judge, which led to the Court of Appeal examining his findings on two periods of time where the judge had found a breach of the Prison Service's duty of care. The Court of Appeal said that the duty of care on the Prison Service must be to make reasonable arrangements for provision of dental treatment. That provision was not of course limited to emergency treatment, but had to encompass such treatment as other citizens were entitled to receive on the NHS. A hard and fast policy of "*one dentist take it or leave it*" was unacceptable. That was not to say that it was unreasonable to have only one dentist generally available. But reasonable arrangements had to include the possibility of alternative provision in particular circumstances.

The Court of Appeal would however reduce the award of pain and suffering to £25,000.

Razumas v Ministry of Justice [2018] EWHC 215 (QB) – **responsibility of a public/private organization for medical care**

The Claimant brought an action for clinical negligence against the Ministry of Justice. He had first been imprisoned in 2010. Towards the end of 2010, following a fall in Pentonville prison, the Claimant developed a cancerous lump on the inner side of his left calf. It was not until August 2013 that the cancer was diagnosed, some three years after his first complaint. An above knee amputation was performed on the 3rd November 2013. He initially sought to bring a claim against the prison healthcare providers who had failed to diagnose the tumour. He approached both private companies who had provided the healthcare in the prisons where he was located and NHS England. No-one was willing to accept responsibility for those who had treated him. On the 31st May 2016, the Claimant sent a Letter of Claim to the Defendant. That letter identified the various alleged breaches by the health care professionals, indicated that none were willing to accept responsibility, and instead intimated a claim against the Ministry of Justice.

The claim was based on a direct duty of care on the prison service, a non-delegable duty of care for the care provided by the health care professionals and for vicarious liability for those health care professionals. Proceedings were issued against the Defendant in August 2016. Later the Claimant amended his claim to include a breach of his rights under Article 3 of the European Convention on Human Rights with reliance also being placed on Article 13

The case came before Mr Justice Cockerill, who said that the question was whether in this case, the negligence was the responsibility of the Ministry of Justice, which had overall responsibility for the prisons in which he was incarcerated, and whether the claim was barred by reason of the Claimant's own actions or whether it was the responsibility of the local Primary Care Trust ("PCT") (now NHS England). There were also a number of subsidiary issues including one as to whether his treatment was in breach of the Human Rights Act 1998.

The Defendant argued that whilst the relevant governor of a prison was responsible for the operation of the prison, it was not responsible for the delivery of healthcare. Primary healthcare was provided by the Primary Care Trust either by itself directly, or by the party with whom it had entered a general medical services contract to provide that service. Looking at the statutory backdrop, only a Primary Care Trust within the National Health Service could incur tortious liabilities arising out of the exercise of its functions. The Defendant relied on a number of statutory provisions, in particular paragraph 16 of Schedule 3 to the National Health Services Act 2006 which dealt with the rights and liabilities of Primary Care Trusts.

Prior to November 2007, section 7 of the Prison Act 1952 required every prison to have a medical officer. This requirement was repealed by section 25 of the Offender Management Act 2007; the explanatory note to that Act indicated that this became the responsibility of the Department of Health and the NHS. Prior to 1st January 2010, rule 20(1) of the Prison Rules 1999 provided:

> *"The medical officer of a prison shall have the care of the health, mental and physical, of the prisoners in that prison".*

This rule was amended by the Prison and Young Offender Institution (Amendment) Rules 2009. It now provided that:

> *"The governor must work in partnership with local health care providers to secure the provision to prisoners of access to the same quality and range of services as the general public receives from the National Health Service".*

Section 249(1) of the National Health Service Act 2006 provided:

> *"In exercising their respective functions, NHS bodies (on the one hand) and the prison service (on the other) must co-operate with one another with a view to improving the way in which those functions are exercised in relation to securing and maintaining the health of prisoners"*

Cockerill J said that the change in the statutory legislation did not operate as a blanket ban to bar an action against anyone other than a PCT. However, there had been a change in the way that healthcare had been delivered in prisons, which was relevant to the Claimant's claim. The new process for handling prisoners' health was initially set out in Prison Service Order PSO 3100. Funding for prison healthcare had been transferred to the Department of Health on the 1st April 2003 and the budget and responsibility were to be transferred to the PCTs over a 3 to 5-year period. Once funding had been transferred, the role of the governor would change from being responsible for healthcare to having, "*important responsibilities for working in partnership with local NHS to support the delivery of good quality, needs-based health services to prisoner*" according to the relevant guidance. Other statutory provisions and guidance outlined that change of responsibility. In this case, personnel who provided prison healthcare were not employed by the prison but by the PCT or the party with whom the PCT had contracted. One of the doctors in this case was under contract to Care UK, which was itself under contract to the PCT. Their medical training, monitoring and quality control was, as a matter of contract the responsibility of their employer and the PCT. So too were disciplinary aspects, evaluation of their performance, dismissal and promotion.

Nonetheless, Cockerill J concluded that the Defendant did owe the Claimant a direct duty of care although it was not the duty for which the Claimant contended, but a more limited duty.

- That duty extended to matters that arose because a prisoner was in custody; so, a duty did exist to take care as to a safe environment, and also as to the less obvious risks such as that of suicide which had been found to be linked to the state of custody.
- The duty also extended to matters relating to access to healthcare. So, if a PCT made provision for GP services for a prison, but the governor failed to put in place arrangements to enable the prisoners to attend the GPs at all, a duty owed by the Defendant would have been breached.
- There was a duty as to oversight of systems (e.g. regarding discharge routines and filling in of the medical part of Prison Escort Record forms).
- There was a duty to raise and seek solutions to identified problems as part of the clinical governance process.
- There was a duty to actively ensure communication of appointments (inferentially even those not actually known to custodial staff).

Regrettably this was insufficient to assist the Claimant on the facts of this case, as there was no custodial part of the relationship which went wrong, and there was no part of the oversight of systems which had been established to be deficient. At the relevant points in time it was the healthcare providers who committed the breach.

The next question was whether there was a non-delegable duty of care. Cockerill J said that the question of non-delegable duty came into play if there was a duty owed but there was no actual breach by the Defendant – because he had entrusted the relevant care to someone else. Consequently, if there was a non-delegable duty of care, then the Defendant might still be liable because the duty of the healthcare provider became the duty of the prison service. Cockerill J referred to two recent cases in which the test for a non-delegable duty had been set out in ***Woodland v Swimming Teachers Association and Others [2014] AC 537.*** The problem for the Claimant was that there had to be a nexus between the control of the Claimant by the Defendant and the purpose of that control/placing, and the care inherent in that relationship. That facet could be easily seen in a hospital, as regards healthcare – a patient gave himself over to the hospital for the very purpose of healthcare. However, the reason for the prisoner being in the hands of the prison was not for reasons of healthcare. Healthcare was not (at least since 2003) part of the prison institution's mainstream (or essential) function.

Reference was made to the decision of Coulson J in ***GB v Home Office [2015] EWHC 819 (QB). 155*** and the preceding judgment of Mr Justice Supperstone in ***Christina Morgan v Ministry of Justice and Another [2010] EWHC 2248 (QB)*** (see above). Cockerill J said that the legislative backdrop in ***GB*** was entirely different. In that case there was an express provision in Rule 33 of the Detention Centre Rules that "*Every detention centre shall have a medical practitioner.... Every detention centre shall have a health care team.*" Thus, healthcare was an essential part of the relationship undertaken between detainee and detention centre. Here it was not. There was also a specific factual context for imputing a duty. As for the case of ***Morgan***, Cockerill J did not think that this case was wrongly decided. The judge in that case, Supperstone J had given a detailed summary of the same complicated statutory position, that Cockerill J had had cited to him and he had come to the same conclusion.

Moreover, the Defendant was not vicariously liable for the healthcare professionals. Cockerill J referred a number of cases including ***Cox v Ministry of Justice [2014] EWCA Civ 132***. He could not see how the Claimant's case met the hurdles of the relevant test in those cases.

Although it was no longer relevant to his decision, Cockerill J dealt with the Defendant's submissions that the Claimant's own conduct had amounted to an intervening cause (in failing to seek medical treatment when he had the opportunity). There were two periods, the 11th January to the 4th April 2011 and again between the 3rd August 2011 and the 9th July 2012 when the Claimant was not in prison. The Defendant submitted that in these periods the Claimant did not seek medical treatment and that this was unreasonable and so broke the causative connection between any earlier negligence and the effects of a failure to treat prior to his return to prison in July 2012. On the evidence, Cockerill J accepted that submission. It seemed likely that the Claimant's reasons for his conduct for doing so was that he did not want to bring himself to the attention of the authorities, given that he had reverted to criminal behaviour. That might be understandable (as was argued on his behalf) on an empathetic level but it was not however, as a matter of law, reasonable behaviour. His actions therefore amounted to an intervening cause, which prevented recovery for any established breach.

The human rights claim related to a breach between 2011 and 2013, and so prima facie it was past the one-year time limit. The claim had been first raised in 2018, and Cockerill J would not extend time. In any event, human rights were not engaged. The breaches complained of were in essence medical matters. The complaint was not made about anything to do with the custody of the Claimant – the matters which went to make up the particulars of the human rights claim related to pain, to lack of medical information and lack of therapeutic strategy. These were not even affected by custody. The failures were healthcare failures and the correct Defendants to this claim, as to the common law claim, were prima facie the relevant healthcare entities. Moreover, the nature of any such breach did not meet the test of minimum severity set out in *Grant and Gleaves v The Ministry of Justice [2011] EWHC 3379 QB.*

5.10 Wrongful detention cases

In the cases below, I have tried to illustrate the principles that the courts apply to actions for false imprisonment. As we saw in Chapter Four, false imprisonment requires the fact of imprisonment and the absence of lawful authority. The absence of lawful authority will generally be the court's main focus and once established, there will be a claim. However, as we will see, a claim may result in only nominal damages because the court may conclude that even though due process was not followed, detention would have resulted even if it had been.

Detention whilst in prison can be false imprisonment

Racz v Home Office [1994] 2 AC 45

The Claimant alleged that whilst a prisoner, he was assaulted by hospital officers in the hospital wing, stripped of his clothing and then put inside a strip cell for two days. His claim for false imprisonment was defended on the grounds that he was already lawfully confined as a prisoner, and consequently it was argued that he could not bring a claim for false imprisonment simply by reason of being moved from one type of confinement to another. The House of Lords said such a claim was possible.

Toumia v Evans The Times 1 April 1999.

The Claimant alleged that prison officers who had failed to let him and other prisoners out of their cells because they were attending a union meeting were liable in false imprisonment and misfeasance in public office. The action had been struck out but the prisoner's appeal was allowed and his case was allowed to proceed to trial. The Court of Appeal said that it was at least arguable that a prison officer who deliberately locks a prisoner in his cell contrary to the orders of the governor will be guilty of the tort of false imprisonment. The court recognised that it might be different where the officer's action was negative in the sense that it was a refusal to obey the governor's order to unlock the cell but held that that was arguable as well. It also held that it was arguable that there was no difference of substance between a prison officer refusing a direct order and a more general refusal to carry out normal duties which included unlocking the prisoners. So, it was also arguable that it would be false imprisonment if a prison officer, acting without the authority of the governor, failed or refused to unlock the cells in accordance with normal routine.

The Prison Officers Association v Iqbal [2009] EWCA Civ 1312

The Claimant was a Category C prisoner. Following a deterioration in the relationship between the Prison Officers Association ("POA") and the Prison Service over pay, the POA decided in August 2007 to call a national strike. This resulted in the Claimant remaining in his cell during the period of the strike – around one day. The trial judge granted a declaration that the Claimant had been falsely imprisoned for some six hours and assessed damages at £5. The POA appealed.

The Court of Appeal referred to the decision of the House of Lords in ***R v Deputy Governor of Parkhurst Prison, Ex p Hague [1992] 1 AC 58***, where the court said that that prisoner serving his sentence had no claim for false imprisonment against a prison governor or officers acting with his authority and in good faith.

However, in this case, the Governor had custody of the prisoners and she actually authorised the specific imprisonment complained of by the Claimant, confining all prisoners at the Prison to their cells. Accordingly, as the person in whose custody the Claimant was placed was not falsely imprisoning him, the officers whose strike caused him to remain in his cell could not be liable either. It would be a very different matter if prison officers positively locked up a prisoner in a cell, when the governor had given the officers clear instructions to let him enjoy recreational activity within the prison, then, particularly if the officers had acted in bad faith, they should be liable for false imprisonment. The appeal would be granted.

AYZ v Home Office [2018] EWHC 2914 (QB) – explanation of the "*Hardial Singh*" principles

This judgment in this case provides a very good up to date summary of the law on these types of wrongful detention cases. The Claimant entered the UK in mid November 2005, aged 14, to be reunited with his mother, who had been granted asylum on the basis of her political affiliations in August 2004. The Claimant was granted indefinite leave to enter the United Kingdom and his passport stamped accordingly upon arrival. Between 2007 and 2012, the Claimant built up a serious criminal record, receiving 15 convictions for 22 offences. In August 2011, the Claimant was arrested and remanded in custody for offences of violent disorder and aggravated robbery during the August 2011 London riots. Having pleaded guilty, he was given a notice of deportation and then detained allegedly unlawfully by the immigration authorities between 9 July 2013 and 1 October 2015.

The judge summarized the principles in the case of ***R (on the application of Singh) v Governor of Durham Prison [1984] 1 WLR 704 (QB)*** known as the ***Hardial Singh*** principles.

- The government must intend to deport the person and can only use the power to detain for that purpose;

- The deportee may only be detained for a period that is reasonable in all the circumstances;

- If before the expiry of the reasonable period, it becomes apparent that the government will not be able to effect deportation within that reasonable period, he should not seek to exercise the power of detention;

- The government should act with reasonable diligence and expedition to effect removal.

In this case, the court concluded that the government had not breached the ***Hardial Singh*** principles.

In *R (Hemmati) v Secretary of State for the Home Department [2018] EWCA Civ 2122*, the Court of Appeal by a majority that the Hardial Singh principles and the Secretary of State's published policy in Chapter 55 of its Enforcement Instructions and Guidance did not satisfy the requirements of Article 23 and Article 2(n) of the Dublin III Regulation (Regulation (EU) No. 604/2013. Briefly "Dublin III" is a European Union Regulation relating to the detention of an individual for the purpose of transfer to another Member State, and it is used where an asylum seeker arrives in a European Union Member State having already made an application for asylum in another Member State. The regulation allows a Member State to transfer the asylum seeker back to the first Member State in which he or she make their application. The Home Office's Enforcement Instructions and Guidance sets out its policy in relation to detention pending removal.

R (Lumba) v Secretary of State for the Home Department [2011] UKSC 12 – Power to detain foreign nationals under immigration powers unlawfully exercised – but only nominal damages awarded

Two foreign nationals, who had been convicted in the UK of a number of serious offences, were detained under immigration powers. The UK Supreme Court examined the principles of unlawful detention and in particular the ***Hardial Singh*** principles. The Home Office was liable to both Claimants in the tort of false imprisonment on the grounds that it unlawfully exercised the statutory power to detain them pending deportation because she applied an unpublished policy which was inconsistent with her published policy. However, they were only entitled to nominal damages because, if the Home Office had acted lawfully and applied the published policy, it was inevitable that both Claimants would have been detained.

R v Governor of Brockhill Prison ex p Evans [2000] UKHL 48 – Mistake in calculating automatic release date

A prison governor calculated a prisoner's automatic release date in accordance with earlier decisions of the Divisional Court in other cases which the Home Office and the governor thought that they were bound to follow. The prisoner successfully challenged these court rulings, and established as a matter of law that she had been kept in prison 59 days beyond what was subsequently held to be her previous release date. The House of Lords said merely because the prisoner was thought to be lawfully detained, that was not a sufficient justification for the tort of false imprisonment even if based on rulings of the court. Consequently, the prison governor was liable for false imprisonment, despite acting in good faith.

The mistake of the Prison Service is to be distinguished from a judicial mistake made by a judge in sentencing a prisoner. In ***Quinland v Governor of HM Prison Belmarsh [2002] EWCA Civ 174*** the sentencing judge indicated a sentence of two years and six months when he should have indicated three months less. The Court of Appeal held that the claim was barred by Section 2(5) of the Crown Proceedings Act 1947. The difference between this case and that in the **Evans** case above was that in ***Quinland***, the governors made no arithmetical or other error.

R (Francis) v Ministry of Justice [2012] EWCA Civ 1200 – Continuing detention was lawful even if discretion to release on Home Detention Curfew was unlawfully exercised

HDC is a scheme whereby prisoners are released early on curfew, which is monitored by the prisoner wearing an electronic device (a tag). The scheme was introduced in 1999 as a result of section 33A of the Criminal Justice Act 1991 (added by the Crime and Disorder Act 1998). The later statutory framework is provided for by section 246 of the Criminal Justice Act 2003.

This was a judicial review concerned with the lawfulness of the Justice Secretary's refusal on the 13th October 2009 to release a foreign national prisoner on Home Detention Curfew. The date on which ordinarily she was eligible for HDC was the 27th July 2009, 135 days before the 8th December 2009, the point at which she was entitled to be released on licence at the half way mark in her sentence. As a foreign national prisoner, however, she could be detained under immigration powers for deportation. The Secretary of State decided that she was liable to deportation on the 11th November 2009.

The Claimant sought public law relief and damages for false imprisonment. She also said that her detention constituted the tort of false imprisonment under domestic law and a breach of Article 5(1) of the European Convention on Human Rights.

The Divisional Court said that even if the Justice Secretary's refusal of her application for HDC was an unlawful exercise of his discretion, the prisoner's detention during the relevant period continued to be a detention pursuant to a sentence lawfully passed. It was therefore neither tortious under domestic law nor in breach of Article 5.1, which excluded the lawful detention of a person after conviction by a competent court. A person sentenced to a determinate sentence of imprisonment was required by law to serve the requisite custodial period, subject to the Justice Secretary's discretion to allow earlier release. A breach of the Justice Secretary's public law duty in the exercise of that discretion did not affect the continuing validity of the sentence or the length of the requisite custodial period.

The Court of Appeal agreed with that decision.

***McCreaner v Ministry of Justice [2014] EWHC 569 (QB)* – Home Detention Curfew ("HDC") – detention by reason of negligence**

This is a long and complex judgment, but again, it is useful because it demonstrates the use of different types of claims, one of which (detention by means of negligence) actually succeeded.

The Claimant, a former prisoner claimed that he was not released under Home Detention Curfew ("HDC") as he should have been, through the fault of the Ministry of Justice. He claimed for false imprisonment, trespass to the person, negligence and breach of human rights. In June 2010, the Supreme Court decision in ***Noone [2010] UKSC 30; [2010] 1 WLR 1743*** was handed down. The effect of that decision was that the Claimant (and many other prisoners) became entitled to HDC earlier than they had been under the old regime. The Claimant claimed that if his sentence had been lawfully calculated and the discretion lawfully exercised as to HDC release he would have been released on HDC on the 1st July 2010. He said that the Ministry of Justice failed to make the correct and lawful calculation which led to his spending some 4 months (119 days) longer than he should have in prison.

In relation to false imprisonment, Mr Justice Cranston said that public law error in calculating a prisoner's release date could mean that the Ministry of Justice was unable to justify imprisonment and the tort of false imprisonment would be established. Public law error would include not acting in accordance with a proper understanding of the law and the wrongful exercise of a discretion. However, the problem in this case was that although up until the 30th June 2010 the Ministry of Justice calculated the Claimant's HDC release date in accordance with a policy which the Supreme Court decision in **Noone** held was unlawful, that did not matter because the Claimant did not become eligible for HDC under the lawful policy until the 1st July 2010. Consequently, the 1st July 2010 was the earliest date on which he could become entitled to HDC.

After the 1st July 2010 those detaining him knew that the policy was unlawful. However, prisoners like the Claimant continued to be held, not under what was now an unlawful policy but until their lawful release dates could be calculated. There was a delay on the part of the Prison Service in calculating what precisely was the Claimant's correct HDC release date in light of the **Noone** case. That certainly led to the Claimant's imprisonment beyond the 1st July which subsequently a lawful calculation concluded was the date from which he was eligible to be released.

However, delay of itself did not constitute public law error. The error in the present case could not be said to constitute an error of law because, after the 1st July 2010, the Claimant was held not under the old policy but pursuant to the court's sentence until his correct eligibility date could be calculated. Detention could not amount to false imprisonment if it was imposed pursuant to the sentence of a court. At no time prior to the 13th November 2010 did this Claimant have a legal right to be released from prison.

In relation to the claim for negligence, Cranston J said that up until early September 2010, none of the Ministry of Justice's actions could give rise to an action in negligence. He referred to the case of ***Rice v Secretary of State for Trade and Industry [2007] EWCA Civ 289*** where the court said that a statute containing broad target duties owed to the public at large, and which did not itself confer on individuals a right of action for breach of statutory duty, was unlikely to give rise to a common law duty of care, breach of which would support a claim by an individual for damages. Such a public law duty was enforceable, if it was justiciable at all, only by judicial review.

The Claimant's situation had changed in early September 2010. The prison had finally decided that the Claimant was eligible for HDC, and indeed that he had been eligible from the 1st July 2010. At that point it had assumed a responsibility to him to complete the final stage of the process associated with his release in accordance with government policy. However, as at September 2010, it was almost another 2 months before he was released. In the view of Cranston J, the prison was at fault in not following the Ministry of Justice guidance sooner. If they had not been in breach of duty, then at least 6 weeks could have been shaved off the period for the Claimant's release on HDC. Consequently, the Claimant was entitled to damages for 6 weeks detention until his final release on HDC in late October 2010.

In relation to misfeasance in public office, the Claimant alleged that the prison officers for whom the Ministry of Justice was vicariously liable, committed misfeasance in public office as a consequence. Cranston J referred to the decision in ***Three Rivers DC v Bank of England (No 3)***

[2003] 2 AC 1. There was no evidential basis on which the Claimant could allege that any prison officer or anyone else had the state of mind, subjective recklessness, necessary to establish untargeted malice and so the misfeasance claim must fail.

In relation to human rights, the Claimant contended that he was a victim of the acts of a public authority. Three Convention rights were invoked: Articles 8, 5 and 14. Cranston J said that the claim must fail in this court in the light of the Court of Appeal decision in ***R (on the application of Francis) v Secretary of State for Justice [2012] EWCA Civ 1200***. The court held that an Article 8 claim could not lie when imprisonment was lawful. That put paid to the claim in relation Article 5 (the Claimant's detention was arbitrary). In relation to Article 14 (discrimination) Cranston J said that in ***R (Clift) v Secretary of State for the Home Department [2006] UKHL 54*** the House of Lords held that the nature of an individual's sentence did not amount to "other status" in Article 14 and that a prisoner could not rely on the type of sentence imposed on him in order to found a claim under it.

5.11 Human rights breaches

Keenan v United Kingdom [2001] ECHR 242 – death in prison

The Applicant alleged that her son, Mark Keenan, had died from suicide in prison due to a failure by the prison authorities to protect his life (Article 2 of the European Convention), that he had suffered inhuman and degrading treatment due to the conditions of detention imposed on him (Article 3) and that she had no effective remedy in respect of her complaints (Article 13).

The European Court of Human Rights considered the various legal remedies available to prisoners in the UK. This included the complaints procedure, the Prison Ombudsman, judicial review, various tortious causes of action, such as negligence, assault and misfeasance in public office as well as the inquest procedure. Having examined all of the evidence, the court found that there had been no breach of Article 2 (failure to protect life).

However, they did find a breach of Article 3. The lack of effective monitoring of Mark Keenan's condition and the lack of informed psychiatric input into his assessment and treatment disclosed significant defects in the medical care provided to a mentally ill person known to be a suicide risk. The belated imposition on him in those circumstances of a serious disciplinary punishment – seven days' segregation in the punishment block and an additional twenty-eight days to his sentence imposed two weeks after the event and only nine days before his expected date of release, was not compatible with the standard of treatment required in respect of a mentally ill person. Consequently, it must be regarded as constituting inhuman and degrading treatment and punishment within the meaning of Article 3 of the European Convention.

Article 13 of the European Convention guaranteed the availability at the national level of a remedy to enforce the substance of the Convention right. Here the European Court said that Mark Keenan was not in a fit mental state to make use of any available remedy when he was still alive. Turning to the remedies available after his death, the inquest did not provide a remedy for determining the liability of the authorities for any alleged ill-treatment or for providing compensation. The European Court was not persuaded that a finding of negligence by the UK courts by itself would be capable of furnishing effective redress for the Applicant's complaints. It did not accept that adequate damages would have been recoverable or that legal aid would have been available to pursue them. Mark Keenan's anguish and fear (in the absence of any psychiatric injury) would not have been regarded as "injury" in the sense recognised by UK domestic law. Furthermore, the Applicant, as the mother of an adult child and a non-dependant, was unable to claim damages under the Fatal Accidents Act 1976 on her own behalf. Consequently, there was a breach of Article 13.

Compensation of £10,000 would be awarded, £3,000 to the Applicant and £7,000 to the estate of Mark Keenan.

Wainwright v United Kingdom [2006] ECHR 807 – wrongful strip search of prison visitors

The Applicants were a mother and her son who attended Armley Prison, Leeds, to visit the mother's son. On arrival they were approached by prison officer and taken away to be strip searched as it was suspected that they were carrying drugs. They brought a claim for trespass to the person against the Home Office, which succeeded at first instance. The Home Office appealed and the Court of Appeal decided that no wrongful act had been committed by the prison officers (save for a battery against the visiting son). That judgment was upheld by the House of Lords. The Applicants brought their claim to the European Court of Human Rights under Articles 3, 8 (right to family life) and 13 of the European Convention.

The European Court found no violation of Article 3, but they did find a violation of Article 8 and 13. The court said that the Applicants were exercising their Article 8 rights to see their relative. There was no direct evidence to connect them with any smuggling of drugs into the prison, in particular as this was the first time that they had visited the prison. The searching of visitors might be considered as a legitimate preventive measure, but the application of such a highly invasive and potentially debasing procedure to persons who were not convicted prisoners or under reasonable suspicion of having committed a criminal offence had to conducted with rigorous adherence to procedures and all due respect to their human dignity.

In relation to Article 13, the Applicants had taken domestic proceedings seeking damages for the searches but had been unsuccessful, save as regards the instance of battery on the Second Applicant. The amount of compensation awarded by the domestic courts was not so derisory as to raise issues of the effectiveness of the redress. As regards the other objectionable elements of the strip searches, the European Court observed that the House of Lords found that the negligent action disclosed by the prison officers did not ground any civil liability, in particular as there was no general tort of invasion of privacy. In these circumstances, the Court found that the Applicants did not have available to them a means of obtaining redress for the interference with their rights under Article 8 of the Convention.

£3000 was awarded to each Applicant.

Grant & Gleaves v The Ministry of Justice [2011] EWHC 3379 (QB) – **the threshold for a claim**

These were two lead cases out of some 550 claims made, mainly in respect of conditions at HMP Albany and HMP Long Lartin. Those two actions were tried by Mr Justice Hickinbottom. Claims were made under Articles 3 and 8 of the European Convention. A civil claim for trespass to the person was upheld at first instance, but the Home Office appealed and the case went before the Court of Appeal who said that the prison officers had committed had no wrongful act, and they were entitled to undertake the search.

The main analysis and findings of the judgment were as follows :-

- The authorities established, clearly and firmly, that a high level of suffering was required to trigger Article 3. It was engaged only where there had been resulting *"...intense physical or mental suffering"* (***Pretty v United Kingdom [2002] 35 EHRR 1***) or where the court has found the treatment of an individual has *"adversely affected his or her personality"* (***Kalashnikov v Russia [2003] 36 EHRR 34***). The test with regard to minimum severity was an objective test, to be determined on the basis of all relevant circumstances, including the effects that the treatment or conditions are likely to have upon a person with the attributes of the victim. Imprisonment as a legitimate punishment inherently involved a degree of suffering.

- A requirement for a prisoner to urinate or defecate into a bucket was not of itself degrading and a violation of Article 3.

- There was no foundation for any complaint in respect of prison conditions at HMP Albany outside the sanitation scheme, e.g. in respect of cell size, lighting and ventilation. Nor was there any foundation for any complaint in respect of the day time sanitation system.

- Prisoners were not obliged to have any waste in their cell for any substantial period. In terms of emptying the bucket, there were sluice facilities and cleaning materials (cleaning solution, brushes and disinfectant) on each landing; and prisoners were given instructions in how to use, and empty, the bucket.

- There was no evidence that the regime caused any material additional risk to the health or well-being of prisoners.

- There was no evidence that the Claimants in the lead cases had suffered any distress or other harm as a result of the regime.

- Neither of the lead Claimants had any disability.

- Article 8 could not be relied upon simply because a claim fell below the Article 3 threshold; and that Article 8, even if engaged, was not breached in these cases, because the regime did not substantively lower the dignity of the prisoners and their privacy was adequately respected.

An attempt by a prisoner at HMP Long Lartin to distinguish his case from that of ***Grant and Gleaves*** failed in ***Kelly v Ministry of Justice [2014] EWHC 3440 (QB).***

R (on the application of Scarfe and Others) v Governor of HMP Woodhill and Another [2017] EWHC 1194 (Admin) –
systemic failure to prevent deaths

The Claimants sought to challenge what they described as "*the Defendants' failures to comply with their public law, common law and Article 2*

ECHR duties to protect prisoners at HMP Woodhill from suicide", failures which they contended were "ongoing". The relief they sought was a declaration that the Defendants had breached those duties and an order requiring them to comply with the mandatory provisions of national prison policy. 7.Also agreed are the national policies which apply. Those national policies were Prison Service Instruction ("PSI") 64/2011 entitled "Management of Prisoners at risk of harm to self, to others and from others (Safer Custody)" and PSI 03/2001 relating to responses to medical emergencies. The background to the case was that had been eighteen self-inflicted deaths in HMP Woodhill since 2013. There were five self-inflicted deaths at the prison in 2015 and seven in 2016. These represented both the highest rate, and the highest number, of self-inflicted deaths in any prison in the entire prison estate. Reports were been produced from the Prisons and Probation Ombudsman for England and Wales ("the PPO") and from the Coroner in relation to inquests that had taken place.

Mr Justice Garnham said that the critical question was whether the Claimants had established that the suicides at HMP Woodhill, or some of them, were the result of a systemic failure by the prison as opposed to an operational failure, i.e. one mistake in each case. Garnham J said that viewed analytically, there had been a series of distinct but separate operational mistakes in suicide prevention at HMP Woodhill. Their frequency did not, of itself, demonstrate a failure of the system but instead, that this was a system prone to operational error. Overall, the evidence did not suggest to us that the same mistake was made time and time again. Instead, it demonstrated that different mistakes were made in specific factual circumstances.

Garnham J pointed out that his judgment would not prevent individual relatives of the deceased bringing claims against the Prison Service.

Moreover, even if there was a systemic error, Garnham J was doubtful whether an injunction, or a mandatory order, or a declaration would have been appropriate. The Defendants had acknowledged that, on occasions, operational errors had been made by their staff in dealing with those at risk of suicide and had sought to prevent those mistakes being repeated. The problem with the Claimants' case was that it looked as though they were saying that "something must be done" without identifying what could be done. A remedy of the sort proposed by the Claimants would serve little purpose.

LW and Others v Sodexo and Another [2019] EWHC 367 (Admin)

Four Claimants detained at HMP Peterborough brought judicial reviews in relation to a series of five alleged illegal strip searches undertaken by Sodexo Limited, a private company that ran HMP Peterborough. One of the Claimants was a transgender prisoner who was born female but was in the process of transitioning to male. The other three Claimants were female.

Sodexo admitted that all of the searches constituted a breach of the relevant Prison Service Instruction, PSI 07/2016, "Searching the Person" and Article 8 of the European Convention on Human Rights. It also admitted a breach by it of its positive obligations under Article 8 of the European Convention and that there was a systemic failure by it to implement PSI 07/2016. It denied any breach of Article 3 of the Convention, either as to the positive or negative obligations that it imposed. The claim for damage had been remitted to the County Court. However, all of Claimants still wanted to obtain declaratory relief against the Ministry of Justice. They alleged that the Ministry of Justice failed to provide adequate and effective safeguards at HMP Peterborough at the relevant time to protect them against violations of Articles 3 and 8 of the Convention.

Mr Justice Knowles examined the legal framework behind private prisons and the power to exercise strip searches, as well as other cases that had come before the courts on the same issue, including the case of ***Wainwright***.

In relation to Article 3, Knowles J held that he was bound by a decision of the Court of Appeal in ***R (BK and RH) v Secretary of State for Justice [2015] EWCA Civ 1259***. In that case the appellants BK and RH were women serving custodial sentences and they were separately subjected to strip searches in their cells. It was conceded that the searches were unlawful. Each of the appellants pursued claims that PSI 67/2011 (the predecessor to PSI 07/2016 infringed Article 3 and Article 8 of the Convention. The Court of Appeal rejected the challenge, holding in relation to Article 3 that PSI 67/2011 provided a framework which was amply compliant with Article 3. The Court of Appeal also noted the absence of any systemic findings. Knowles J said that in the absence of any clear evidence of systemic breaches of Article 3 by Sodexo in this case, he would reject the Claimants' case under Article 3 against the Ministry of Justice. Because the Court of Appeal had held that PSI 67/2011 provided sufficient compliance with Article 3, the same conclusion followed in respect of the replacement policy PSI 07/2016.

In relation to Article 8, the Court of Appeal in ***R (BK and RH)*** had also rejected that claim. However, Knowles J said that the present case was distinguishable because of Sodexo's admitted systemic breaches of relation to PSI 07/2016 and Article 8. This constituted the sort of systemic and significant failings which were absent in ***R (BK and RH)***. Also, there was no question in that case of the absence of the adequate training of staff, which was an important aspect of this case. Moreover, the failings here were not by a single officer, but by at least 12 individual officers involved in one of the searches that took place. Intelligence officers were also involved in tasking the searching officers. These breaches were serious and no adequate reasons had been given for the searches themselves. The Ministry of Justice had a particular obligation to take effective steps to make reasonably sure breaches of this nature did not occur. The Prison Service gave evidence to the effect that they used a "Compliance Checking Tool" to check on Sodexo's performance on a monthly basis. However, this tool referred to the old PSI 67/2011 rather than the new PSI 07/2016. Knowles J said that the measures put in place by the Ministry of Justice to ensure that Sodexo had procedures in place to train its staff properly had failed. If those measures had been effective then staff would have been properly trained and the breaches would not have occurred in a way properly described as systemic. Consequently, Knowles J would order a declaration that Article 8 had been breached by the Ministry of Justice.

CHAPTER SIX
DAMAGES

6.1 Damages for wrongful detention – the basic principles

There are now quite a number of cases on wrongful detention, mainly involving those who have been detained pending potential deportation. The court in the case of ***R (on the application of Diop) v Secretary of State for the Home Department 2018] EWHC*** commented that these cases do not set out any "guidelines" that might be applied in quantifying any award of damages for unlawful immigration detention. Each showed what sum the court has decided that it is appropriate to award as damages on the facts in that particular case. The cases provide some indication of a general level of the amounts that might be awarded, however the court urged a "*more selective approach to the citation of such cases.*"

More recently, in ***R (on the application of Majewski) [2019] EWHC 472 (Admin)*** (which also contains a helpful and up-to-date summary of the law) the court said that the assessment of damages for non-financial loss in unlawful detention claims is neither a mechanical exercise nor precise science. There is no "daily rate", and no tariff which sets the amount of an award. The overall object is to identify an amount of money appropriate to compensate the Claimant for the non-financial loss resulting from unlawful detention. The relevant damage is in the nature of injury to feelings, or the pain and suffering caused by the detention.

The basic principles for awarding damages for wrongful detention or false imprisonment are summarised in the judgment in ***MK (Algeria) v Secretary of State for the Home Department [2010] EWCA Civ 980.*** Three general principles should be borne in mind :-

- The assessment of damages should be sensitive to the facts and the particular case and the degree of harm suffered by the particular Claimant.

- Damages should not be assessed mechanistically by fixing a rigid figure to be awarded for each day of incarceration.

- Whilst obviously the gravity of a false imprisonment is worsened by its length the amount broadly attributable to the increasing passage of time should be tapered or placed on a reducing scale. This is for two reasons: (i) to keep this class of damages in proportion with those payable in personal injury and perhaps other cases; and (ii) because the initial shock of being detained will generally attract a higher rate of compensation than the detention's continuance.

In ***Thompson v Commissioner of Police [1998] QB 498***, the court gave specific guidance to the effect that in a "straightforward case of wrongful arrest and imprisonment" the starting point was likely to be about £500 for the first hour of loss of liberty and a Claimant wrongly detained for 24 hours should for that alone normally be entitled to an award of about £3,000 although it should be borne in mind that this case is now over twenty years old. Practitioners also need to bear in mind the effect of ***Simmons v Castle [2012] EWCA Civ 1039*** which raises the level of general damages by 10% after the 1st April 2013.

Compensatory damages for wrongful detention comprise two elements.

- The first (sometimes referred to as a "basic amount") consists of damages to reflect the fact of detention and the restrictions and deprivations that are the ordinary consequence of any deprivation of liberty. This amount includes compensation for the "first shock" of detention, i.e. damages initially at a higher level for the first hour, and the first 24 hours of detention – and also further compensation for the remaining period of the detention. Damages for the remaining period will be awarded on a progressively reducing scale.

- The second element of compensatory damages reflects any special features of the case in hand that have aggravated the pain and suffering of detention. For example, the circumstances of detention, the Defendant's conduct in the course of the detention, and so on. The object remains compensation, this time directed to any aggravated injury to the claimant's feelings including compensation for any continuing consequences of the detention on the Claimant's health and well-being, which have not already been taken account of in the basic amount. There is no particular threshold for an award of aggravated damages.

6.2 Case law

R (on the application of Jollah) v Secretary of State for the Home Department [2018] EWCA Civ 1260 – the Claimant was made subject to a curfew restriction between the hours of 23.00 and 07.00 for a period between 3 February 2014 and 14 July 2016, pending potential deportation. He claimed successfully for false imprisonment, and the trial judge gave him £4,000 compensation, which was upheld by the Court of Appeal. The trial judge had declined to award aggravated damages and there was no claim for exemplary damages.

NAB v Secretary of State for the Home Department [2011] EWHC 1191 – The Claimant was detained unlawfully for 82 days when it became clear that there was no realistic prospect of his removal within a reasonable period after a period in lawful detention of 30 months. He suffered no initial shock and no disruption to an otherwise normal life when his unlawful detention began, something of which he was unaware. The judge awarded him compensation in May 2011 at a rate of £75 per day, a total of £6,150 but refused to award aggravated or exemplary damages.

R (on the application of Diop) v Secretary of State for the Home Department 2018] EWHC 420 (Admin) –The Claimant was a foreign national offender who was lawfully detained by the Defendant under immigration act powers on the completion of the custodial part of his sentence of imprisonment, the 5th September 2016. On the 10th November 2017, the First Tier Tribunal granted him bail in principle, requiring the Defendant to provide him with initial accommodation within a 14-day period. He brought a claim for wrongful detention. The court found that, had the Defendant acted lawfully, it should have secured bail accommodation for the Claimant by the 10th November 2017 and by that date, there was then no prospect of the Defendant deporting the Claimant within a reasonable period. Consequently, the Claimant's detention from the 10th November 2017 until his eventual release from detention on the 7th December 2017 was unlawful. He had been deprived of his liberty unlawfully for 28 days, although he did not then know that was the case and he suffered no initial shock when he was not released on the 10th November 2017. He knew that he would not then be released even if bail was granted in principle by the First Tier Tribunal, as he knew that he had no bail accommodation. He nonetheless became increasingly frustrated and angry and concerned about when he would be released and be able to see his children in that 14 day period and, although he was pleased when the FTT made a further grant of bail in principle, he felt worse as, until he was told that accommodation had been found for him on the 5th December 2017, he had no idea when he would be released and he was preparing himself for the possibility of his detention continuing for much longer. The judge awarded the Claimant £9,000 to include aggravated damages. There was no award for exemplary damages.

R (on the application of Majewski) [2019] EWHC 472 (Admin) – The Claimant was unlawfully detained at an immigration detention centre between 14 March 2017 and 20 April 2017, a period of 38 days. He was awarded £14,800. The court refused to award aggravated or exemplary damages.

R (Belfken) v Secretary of State for the Home Department [2017] EWHC 1834 (Admin) – The Claimant was unlawfully detailed from the 12th July 2016 until the 3rd May 2017 – over nine months. The trial judge took into account several factors. He found that the Claimant had been uncooperative and obstructive with the authorities, but he would not put the degree of obstruction he had displayed in the same category as the Claimant in ***NAB v Secretary of State for the Home Department [2011] EWHC 1191***. The judge awarded £40,000. This reflected the length of his unlawful detention; the lack of any aggravating factors, or any egregious conduct on the part of the Home Office and the overall justice of the case. The judge would not award any aggravated or exemplary damages.

R (Mohammed) v Home Office [2017] EWHC 2809 (QB) – The Claimant was a 39 year-old Somali, who was a prolific and violent offender and had spent much of the previous two decades in and out of custody or immigration detention. In November 2017 he was awarded damages for three periods of unlawful immigration detention each of which followed a period of lawful custody: £8,500 for the first period of 41 days; £25,000 for the second period of 139 days; and £45,000 for the third period of 265 days. The first two periods and the first 81 days of the third had been served under a more restrictive prison regime and his detention exacerbated the Claimant's post-traumatic stress disorder. The awards also reflected to some extent the views of the judge about the Defendant's failure to engage seriously with the principles governing lawful detention; the failure to release the Claimant in accordance with the Defendant's policy on receipt of independent medical evidence of torture in the third period; and the Defendant's conduct of the litigation. The award included aggravating features although the judge did not value these separately (see below on aggravated damages).

AXD v Home Office [2016] EWHC 1617 (QB) – The Claimant, a foreign national offender, who had been subject previously to immigration detention on more than one occasion, was detained on the 27th November 2011 on completion of another custodial sentence. His detention became unlawful on the 1st April 2013 by which time he had developed paranoid schizophrenia and he remained unlawfully in detention until his release on the 5th December 2014, a period of 20 months and 5 days. For a considerable part of that period he was locked in a cell in

HMP Woodhill for 21 hours a day with only 30 minutes of fresh air. He also experienced some unpleasant abuse because of his sexual orientation and he was assaulted on one occasion. The judge awarded him £80,000 as a "basic award" in respect of those matters with a further award of "aggravated damages" of £25,000 to reflect the unacceptable delay in the Defendant's decision-making; the sub-optimal treatment for his schizophrenia from July 2013 to May 2014; his eventual release without a proper welfare plan and its consequences; and the Defendant's breach of its duty of candour. He would not award exemplary damages.

6.3 Aggravated damages

If a claim is made based on assault or battery, false imprisonment or misfeasance in public office, then a claim for aggravated damages must be considered.

In ***Commissioner of Police of the Metropolis v Shaw [2012] ICR 464***, Mr Justice Underhill in the Employment Appeal Tribunal summarised the concept of aggravated damages (paragraph 15 of his judgment onwards). He referred to Part II of the Law Commission Report (no. 247) on Aggravated, Exemplary and Restitutionary Damages, which in his judgment, represented the clearest and most comprehensive guide to the law up to 1997.

> *"Although the precise meaning and function of aggravated damages is unclear, the best view, in accordance with Lord Devlin's authoritative analysis in Rookes v Barnard [1964] AC 1129, appears to be that they are damages awarded for a tort as compensation for the plaintiff's mental distress, where the manner in which the defendant has committed the tort, or his motives in so doing, or his conduct subsequent to the tort, has upset or outraged the plaintiff. Such conduct or motive aggravates the injury done to the plaintiff, and therefore warrants a greater or additional compensatory sum."*

Underhill J made three points :-

- Aggravated damages are compensatory in nature and not punitive.
- The features that may attract an award of aggravated damages can be classified under three heads – (a) the manner in which the defendant has committed the tort; (b) the motive for it; and (c) the defendant's conduct subsequent to the tort but in relation to it.
- The features enumerated at (2) above affect the award of compensation because they aggravate the distress caused by the actual wrongful act.

In ***Thompson v Commissioner of Police Metropolis [1998] QB 498*** the Court of Appeal said that aggravated damages can be awarded where there are aggravating features about the case which would result in the plaintiff not receiving sufficient compensation for the injury suffered if the award were restricted to a basic award. Aggravating features can include humiliating circumstances at the time of arrest or any conduct of those responsible for the arrest or the prosecution which shows that they had behaved in a high handed, insulting, malicious or oppressive manner either in relation to the arrest or imprisonment or in conducting the prosecution. Aggravating features can also include the way the litigation and trial are conducted.

In practice, it can be difficult to obtain aggravated damages and extremely difficult to obtain exemplary damages.

By way of example in ***NAB v Secretary of State for the Home Department [2011] EWHC 1191*** the court commented that although there had been a number of awards (and decisions refusing awards) of aggravated damages, little or nothing of principle was added to the principles set out in ***Thompson***, and there was no call for a "parade of learning". In this case, there was no aggravation of the illegality, nothing in the manner in which the detention was continued which added injury to insult, or would otherwise justify an award of aggravated damages. In relation to exemplary damages the court said that what fault it had found on the part of the Home Office consisted of inactivity and drift.

The court did not find any bad faith, malice, fraud, insolence or cruelty. The facts did not amount to "oppressive, arbitrary or unconstitutional action by the servants of government" By comparison, the court referred to another unlawful detention case ***Muuse v Secretary of State for the Home Department*** *[2009] EWHC 1886 (QB)* and addressed on appeal in *[2010[EWCA 453*. In that case £60,000 was awarded to the Claimant to include both aggravated and exemplary damages.

In ***Williams v Tascor Services Limited*** *[2017] EWHC 1461 (QB)* the Defendant was escorting an illegal immigrant onto a removal flight. The Defendant was found to have detained the Claimant in improper circumstances, used unprofessional/possibly racist language, used unreasonable force as well as painful and degrading treatment. Mr Justice Walker awarded £2,000 for the use of force and transient injuries, £12,000 for wrist injuries and £16,000 for exacerbation of PTSD, a total of £30,000 for "ordinary" damages. Aggravated damages were awarded in the sum of £8,000.

Although aggravated damages were awarded separately in the above case and courts continue to adopt that approach, there is guidance from the Court of Appeal that encourages judges to make a global award. The reason is that drawing a sharp distinction between any injury to the Claimant's feelings caused by the wrong itself (which is included in the basic award of damages) and any injury to the Claimant's feelings caused by the manner in which it was committed (to be reflected in an award of aggravated damages) is inevitably arbitrary and is liable to create a risk of double counting. This has led to the recommendation, contained in two decisions of the Court of Appeal – ***Richardson v Howie*** *[2004] EWCA Civ 1127* and ***Choudhary v Martins*** *[2007] EWCA Civ 1379* that the basic and aggravated awards be expressed as one award when judgment is given, rather than being set out separately.

6.4 Exemplary damages

Exemplary or punitive damages are the court's way of telling the Defendant that their wrong does not pay. They are only awarded in those categories of cases identified in ***Rookes v Barnard [1964] AC 1129***. These are :-

- Where the court finds "oppressive, arbitrary or unconstitutional conduct by servants of the Government" which would include the Prison Service.

- Where the Defendant's conduct has been calculated by him to make a profit for himself which may well exceed the compensation payable to the Claimant

- Where expressly authorised by statute.

In ***AB v South West Water Services Ltd [1993] 1 All ER 609*** the court decided that punitive damages could only be awarded for those types of tortious claims for which such damages had been awarded prior to ***Rookes v Barnard*** i.e. false imprisonment, wrongful arrest together with assault and battery. However, in ***Kuddus v Chief Constable of Leicestershire Constabulary [2001] UKHL 29*** the House of Lords decided that punitive damages could be awarded for misfeasance in public office together with potentially other tortious causes of action, which would include negligence. The House of Lords did not express a view on whether exemplary damages could be awarded in discrimination and human rights cases.

There is an obvious overlap between aggravated and exemplary damages, a point made by the Court of Appeal in ***Thompson***. However, in the case of ***Muuse v Secretary of State for the Home Department [2009] EWHC 1886 (QB)*** the court identified a separate award of £27,500 for exemplary damages, and then added it to the basic and aggravated damages award of £25,000 and £7,500, awarding a figure of £60,000. The award of exemplary damages was upheld on appeal.

CHAPTER SEVEN
DEATHS IN PRISON

7.1 Introduction

In January of this year, the Howard League reported the following chilling statistics :-

https://howardleague.org/news/shocking-rise-in-deaths-in-custody/

- The number of prisoners who died by suicide rose by 31% in 2018
- Overall deaths in custody rose by 10% in 2018
- Incidents of self-injury increase by 23%

The prison suicide rate, at 120 deaths per 100,000 people, is about 10 times higher than the rate in the general population. There has also been a rise in the number of deaths in prison that appear to be unexplained.

The law of inquests in relation to deaths in prison is ably set out in Inquests – A Practitioner's Guide at Chapters 18 and 19, to which we referred in Chapter One. Consequently, this Chapter is simply an introduction to the subject with some key points on prison procedures.

7.2 The role of the Coroner

Inquests and the role of the Coroner are governed by the Coroners and Justice Act 2009, the Coroners (Investigations) Regulations 2013 and the Coroners (Inquests) Rules 2013.

Section 5 of the Coroners and Justice Act 2009 says :-

"(1) The purpose of an investigation under this Part into a person's death is to ascertain—

(a) who the deceased was;

(b) how, when and where the deceased came by his or her death;

(c) the particulars (if any) required by the 1953 Act to be registered concerning the death.

(2) Where necessary in order to avoid a breach of any Convention rights (within the meaning of the Human Rights Act 1998 (c. 42)), the purpose mentioned in subsection (1)(b) is to be read as including the purpose of ascertaining in what circumstances the deceased came by his or her death."

Prison Service Instruction PSI 15/2014 specifically refers to the need in certain cases for an Article 2 compliant investigation in cases of serious cases of self-harm or violence.

Regulation 28 of the 2013 Regulations now allows the Coroner to submit a report following an inquest to the relevant authorities, i.e. the Prison Service.

Regulations 12 to 16 of the Coroners (Inquests) Rules 2013 provide for the Coroner to make disclosure and Regulation 13 allows an interested party to ask the Coroner to disclose any document that the Coroner has in his possession. In the case of a death in prison, advance disclosure is absolutely key. Schedule 5 to the 2009 Act sets out the Coroner's powers to require a party to make disclosure of evidence.

Prison Service Instruction PSI 64/2011 sets out what the Prison Service is expected to do, in order to avoid suicides. This is entitled "Management of prisoners at risk of harm to self, to others and from others (Safer Custody)".

PSI 64/2011 expired on the 31st January 2016, but it appears to be the current guidance used by the Prison Service according to their website page dated the 15th May 2019. This page provides a link to guidance published by the National Institute of Care and Excellence published the 10th September 2018 – "*Preventing suicide in community and custodial settings custodial settings*".

www.gov.uk/guidance/suicide-self-harm-prevention-in-prison

Other PSIs may be relevant, such as PSI 16/2015 – Adult Safeguarding in Prisons, PSI 07/2015 – Early Days in Custody, PSI 15/2014 – Investigations and learning following incidents of serious self-harm or serious assaults or PSO 1700 Segregation.

7.3 Article 2

Article 2 of the European Convention on Human Rights provides by Article 2.1:

> *"Everyone's right to life shall be protected by law. No one shall be deprived of his life intentionally save in the execution of a sentence of a court following his conviction of a crime for which the penalty is provided by law."*

As we saw in Chapter Four, it is unlawful for a public authority to act in a way which is incompatible with a Convention right (Section 6 Human Rights Act 1998). This can include a failure to act (Section 6(6)) and in practical terms this means that not only is the Prison Service expected to take measures to prevent suicide, but also where there is a death in custody, the Prison Service is expected to institute an Article 2 compliant investigation.

Prior to the introduction of the Human Rights Act 1998 and the Coroners and Justice Act 2009, the law recognised that deaths in custody should be properly investigated. The case *of **R v HM Coroner for North Humberside and Scunthorpe, Ex parte Jamieson [1995] QB 1*** concerned a prisoner who hanged himself in prison, and the responsibility of prison officers for his welfare. The court said that the Coroner should ensure that the relevant facts were "fully, fairly and fearless investigated."

In ***Keenan v UK [2001] 33 EHRR 38*** (See Chapter Five) the European Court of Human Rights acknowledged that the obligation under Article 2 extended to a duty to prevent suicides in custody where the authorities were on notice of a real and immediate risk to life.

In ***R v Home Office ex parte Amin [2003] UKHL 51***, a young prisoner at Feltham, Zahid Mubarek was murdered by his notoriously violent and racist cell mate. There was a criminal trial, the Prison Service admitted fault and there was also an internal inquiry by the Prison Service, the report from which was disclosed to the deceased's family. There was also a private investigation into racism in the Prison Service. However, the family of Mr Mubarek pressed the Home Office for a public inquiry on the grounds that there had been no public investigation into the acts and/or omissions of Prison Service personnel in which they had been able to participate. They judicially reviewed the Home Office refusal to hold that public inquiry.

Lord Bingham in the House of Lords said that the state's duty to investigate a death in custody was secondary to the duties not to take life unlawfully and to protect life, in the sense that it only arose where a death had occurred or life-threatening injuries had occurred. However, it was not a minor or unimportant duty. There was no inquest in this case, which was very unfortunate, since that could have discharged the state's investigative obligation. The police investigations into the criminal culpability of the cell mate and the Prison Service were, very properly, conducted in private and without participation by the family. There was an Advice Report on which counsel based his advice not to prosecute the Prison Service or any of its members, but whilst this was objective, it raised many unanswered questions and could not discharge the state's investigative duty. The trial of the cell mate for murder was directed solely to establishing his mental responsibility for the killing which he had admittedly carried out. It involved little exploration, such as would occur in some murder trials, of wider issues concerning the death. The internal inquiry conducted by the Prison Service had been undertaken in a conscientious and professional way, but because it was undertaken by a serving official in the Prison Service, that official did not enjoy institutional or hierarchical independence. His investigation was conducted in private and it was not published. There had also been a report from the Commission for Racial Equality, published under the Race Relations Act 1976 which brought additional facts to light but this was necessarily confined to race-related issues, and the inquiry was conducted in private. None of the investigations were capable of discharging the State's obligations under Article 2. The resulting public inquiry can be found at www.gov.uk/government/publications/report-of-the-zahid-mubarek-inquiry.

R v HM Coroner for Western District of Somerset ex parte Middleton [2004] UKHL 10 raised a question, different to that raised in **Amin.** Two other questions related to the current inquest legislation, the Coroners Act 1988 and the Coroners Rules 1984 which has now been replaced. The background to the case was the suicide of Colin Middleton, who hanged himself while in custody in HMP Bristol. An inquest took place, the verdict of which was quashed and at the second inquest, the verdict of the jury was that Mr Middleton had killed himself whilst the balance of his mind was disturbed. The jury dealt not only with the immediate circumstances of the death, but also the background to Mr Middleton's death. After the close of the evidence, the Coroner ruled that the issue of "neglect" should not be left to the jury, and he summed up accordingly. Mr Middleton's family challenged that verdict.

The case came before the House of Lords. The key question was – what, if anything, did the European Convention on Human Rights require (by way of verdict, judgment, findings or recommendations) of a properly conducted official investigation into a death involving, or possibly involving, a violation of Article 2?

The House of Lords said that where an inquest was the instrument by which the state sought to discharge its investigative obligation, an explicit statement, however brief, of the jury's conclusion on the central issue was required. The inquest might not establish liability but it had to furnish the applicant with the possibility of establishing the responsibility of the prison authorities, and it had to be an investigation capable of leading to the identification and punishment of those responsible for the deprivation of life. Therefore, to meet the procedural requirement of Article 2 an inquest ought ordinarily to culminate in an expression, however brief, of the jury's conclusion on the disputed factual issues at the heart of the case.

In ***Amin***, the House of Lords said that a similar obligation may arise under Article 2 when the victim does not die but has sustained "life threatening injuries". Two examples of such cases where the courts held that the Article 2 obligation would arise are ***R (D) v Secretary of State for the Home Department [2005] EWHC*** and ***R(JL) v Secretary of State for the Home Department [2006] EWHC 2558 (Admin).***

CHAPTER EIGHT
PROCEDURAL AND PRACTICAL MATTERS IN LITIGATION

8.1 Introduction

A serving prisoner bringing a claim against, for instance for the Ministry of Justice, faces a number of practical problems, not least of which will be their ability to attend trial to give evidence. At the same time, it is important to realise that the Senior Courts Act 1981 s.69(1) and Rule.26.11 of the Civil Procedure Rules entitle certain types of claim to a trial by jury as opposed to a trial before a judge only. Section 69(1)(b) allows a trial by jury in claims for malicious prosecution or false imprisonment.

8.2 Use of documents produced in criminal proceedings

The Claimant should be entitled to see his/her own witness statement on request. All police forces should have a standard "right of access form" document for making a request for information, which can be found on their respective websites.

In relation to witness statements made by others, generally speaking these should be discloseable either under Checklist 7 to Annex E Prison Service Instruction 31/2015, which we examined in Chapter Three. This provides for various documents to be provided to the Claimant's solicitors in the case of an assault on a prisoner, and it includes statements given to the police.

Otherwise a court order can be sought. ***Frankson v Home Office [2003] EWCA Civ 655*** concerned a number of claims brought by prisoners alleging assaults by prison officers. A prison officer appealed against a decision made pursuant to Rule 31.17 of the Civil Procedure Rules to allow the disclosure of interviews under caution made by him and a number of his colleague during the course of a criminal investigation. The competing arguments were that the prison officers were particularly vulnerable to unfounded allegations made by prisons and that the interview by the police had been undertaken under caution, in circumstances of confidentiality. The prisoners said that they were in a vulnerable position and it is critical that any evidence supporting their claims should be placed before the court. The Court of Appeal said that the issue which fell to be decided was whether the court should exercise its discretion to order disclosure. The court had to balance competing public interests, namely, on the one hand, the public interest of maintaining the confidentiality of those who made statements to the police in the course of a criminal investigation, and, on the other, the public interest of ensuring that the courts tried civil claims on the basis of all the relevant material with a view to achieving a fair and just result. It was the public interest relied on by the prisoners that outweighed the need to maintain confidentiality.

The Court of Appeal considered Rule 31.17 of the Civil Procedure Rules and set out a three-point test :-

- Does the disclosure sought meet the test of relevance?

- Is disclosure necessary in order to dispose fairly of the claim or to save costs? The possibility of finding something must be real and not fanciful.

- Should the court exercise its discretion whether or not to make an order?

Whilst it may be possible to get the police to disclose documents, getting information out of the Crown Prosecution Service may be more difficult as they may contest the Claimant's right to see key documents (for instance the reasons behind a decision made by the CPS not to prosecute prison officers) based on public interest immunity.

8.3 Cummings and Others v Ministry of Justice [2013] EWHC 33 (QB)

The issues above were all examined in this case, which involved multiple prisoners at HMP Frankland. The Claimants were serving prisoners seeking damages (including aggravated and exemplary damages) in assault. All the Claimants contended that they had been racially abused. The First Claimant also alleged misfeasance in public office and malicious prosecution. A counter claim was made against by the Defendant against the Claimant for damage to their cells. Mr Justice Tugendhat dealt with several pre-trial issues, which were the scope of the trial, the mode of trial (whether it should take place before a jury), the manner of attendance on the part of the Claimants and the witnesses and the venue.

The Claimants sought a trial by jury. The First Claimant contended that he had a *prima facie* right to trial by jury in respect of the malicious prosecution allegation and that because the factual basis for his claims for assault and misfeasance, as well as those claims brought by other Claimants were inextricably linked with the facts that supported his claim for malicious prosecution, it would not be feasible or cost-effective to separate the two. This would lead to two trials dealing with substantially overlapping issues, with significant duplication of evidence and costs.

The Claimants also sought to call 33 witnesses with 25 from the Defendant, and that they, the Claimants, should be allowed to attend the trial in person in order to be able fully to participate in their trial by giving evidence in person, hearing the Ministry of Justice's witnesses, and also, critically, being able to give their legal representatives timely instructions on the evidence which they heard.

Relevant and admissible evidence

Tugendhat J dealt with the issue of relevant and admissible evidence. The Claimants' Particulars of Claim included an allegation that the regime at the prison was such that racism on the part of prisoners was actively condoned by staff. The Claimants wanted to adduce evidence from witnesses about the behaviour of inmates and prison officers notwithstanding that it was not similar fact evidence.

It was not similar fact evidence because it did not purport to relate to the actions of any of the prison officers (named or unnamed) whose acts or omissions were complained of in this action. For instance, one of the witnesses was a journalist who stated that in the past he was sentenced to a number of terms of imprisonment in and between 1957 and 1996. He described his experience in those years without identifying any prison or prison officer. His evidence as to HMP Frankland related to letters he had received as a journalist from inmates reporting abuse. He referred in his evidence to a report in The Independent entitled "HMP Frankland's Brutal Regime – the Inside Story". He had never met or spoken to any of the Claimants.

The Defendant said that the parts of the Particulars of Claim in which the evidence of these witnesses had been made should be struck out because the disputed evidence was not similar fact evidence and was not relevant on any other basis. It was accepted that those witnesses for the Claimants who could give direct evidence of the incidents the subject of this action might also give evidence concerning alleged racism at the prison in so far as it is relevant to the assaults in question.

Tugendhat J said that the evidence sought to be adduced was irrelevant on a number of grounds.

- It did not purport to relate to any of the officers (named or unnamed) whose acts or omissions were complained of in this action. The fact that one prison officer committed a racist assault on one prisoner could not fairly be relied on to prove that another prison officer committed a racist assault on a different occasion upon one or other of the Claimants.

- In most instances, the evidence was so vague that it would be impossible for the Defendant to investigate it or attempt to contradict it.

The evidence might be relevant to the Claimant's states of minds if they had wanted to defend the counterclaims for the damage they did to their cells, but they had not defended those counterclaims, and judgment had been entered against them.

It followed that there should be struck out of the witness statements all evidence relating to acts or omissions or other matters alleged to have occurred at any time other than the material times of the incidents that were the subject of the claim.

Mode of Trial

Pursuant to the Senior Courts Act 1981 s.69(1) and the CPR Rule.26.11 the Claimants were entitled to trial with a jury in respect of the claim for malicious prosecution. The issue between the parties was whether the other claims (for assault and battery and misfeasance in public office) should also be tried with a jury.

Tugendhat J said that the claims in this action against officers of the state were all ones of a kind which juries commonly do determine, and which, for well-known reasons, it was in the public interest that there be trial by jury. The issues were all closely linked. There was no interest of justice that would be served by a split trial, or by some of the issues being tried by judge alone. The First Claimant had a statutory right to trial with a jury on the malicious prosecution claim. It would not be in the interests of justice if that claim were to be severed from his other claims.

Attendance at trial

The Claimants were all Category A prisoners serving terms of life imprisonment. The Defendant said that the Claimants and their witnesses could attend by video link, and if they did, then the trial could be held at the Royal Courts of Justice in London. Alternatively, if any of the Claimants or any prisoner witness was to attend, then the venue of any trial should not be the Royal Courts of Justice, but Woolwich Crown Court. This would enable those responsible for security to take appropriate measures, whereas another venue might expose the public to serious risk, and would certainly involve the deployment of more resources in maintaining security.

Tugendhat J said that fairness required that the Claimants give evidence in person, and that they be present in court when the Defendant's witnesses are giving evidence. The court should, however, pay careful regard to the implications in terms both of security and resources. He accepted in principle that the Royal Courts of Justice were unlikely to be a suitable venue.

8.4 Locating and corresponding with a prison or prisoner

Prisons can be found on the Ministry of Justice's website at :-

http://www.justice.gov.uk/contacts/prison-finder

It should be possible to locate a prisoner using Prisoner Location Service. There is a website address which tells you what information is required.

Prisoner Location Service
PO Box 2152
Birmingham
B15 1SD
Fax: 0121 626 3474
Email: prisoner.location.service@noms.gsi.gov.uk
http://www.justice.gov.uk/offenders/prisoner-location-service/

All prisoners have numbers which remain the same wherever they are. It is important to establish that number, if possible. The Service will require the date of the prisoner's conviction and the letter of request should set out clearly the reason for the request.

Whilst this service is very helpful, practitioners should be cautious. It is quite common for inmates to be moved from one prison to another without warning (particularly after they have been first convicted). In theory a letter sent to a prisoner will reach that prisoner eventually provided the correct prisoner number is on the letter.

A prisoner is allowed to correspond with the court and his legal adviser without that correspondence being opened under Rule 39 of the Prison Rules 1999 (as amended). However, that rule refers to correspondence with the court and the prisoner's own legal adviser. Communications to and from the prisoner with other persons are allowed under Rule 34 onwards but they can be restricted "*with a view to securing discipline and good order or the prevention of crime or in the interests of any person.*"

8.5 Section 57 of the Criminal Justice and Courts Act 2015 – the dangers of giving false or exaggerated evidence

We looked at the judgment in ***Razumas v Ministry of Justice*** *[2018] EWHC 215 (QB).* That case involved the alleged healthcare in prison. The claim ultimately failed, but an additional point was made by the Defendant pursuant to Section 57 of the Criminal Justice and Courts Act 2015. The trial judge, Mr Justice Cockerill had found that parts of the Claimant's evidence being false meant that the positive averment and allegation in the Particulars of Claim (and repeated in his evidence) was false to his knowledge. The Defendant said that he had sought to base one of his allegations of negligence on a false assertion that he sought treatment, and this meant that he had been "fundamentally dishonest" in an aspect of his claim and the claim failed pursuant to section 57.

Cockerill J asked himself the following questions :-

- Did the Claimant act dishonestly in relation to the primary claim and/or a related claim? To this the answer must be yes. He had one main claim, and the dishonesty went to one route to succeed on it in full.

- Had he thus substantially affected the presentation of his case, either in respect of liability or quantum, in a way which potentially adversely affected the Defendant in a significant way? Again, the answer must be yes. The argument which he advanced went to an entire factual section and pleaded occasion which would have entitled relief on the main claim.

Consequently, fundamental dishonesty was made out. Section 57 required the court to ask whether substantial injustice would result to the Claimant. Cockerill J said that it could not be right to say that substantial injustice would result in disallowing the claim where a Claimant had advanced dishonestly a claim which if established would result in full compensation.

CHAPTER NINE
FUNDING FOR CLAIMS

9.1 Introduction

The funding of most personal injury claims is undertaken by the use of Conditional Fee Agreements, which will be appropriate for the vast majority of claims backed by legal expenses insurance, unless the solicitors firm opts to fund these risks itself. Legal expenses insurance typically covers the costs of the Claimant's disbursements and the risk of an adverse costs order under Part 36 of the Civil Procedure Rules.

However, there are situations, where a prisoner might be able to obtain legal aid for a personal injury, and we examine that possibility below.

Legal aid for relatives of a deceased prisoner is a vexed subject. Again, in this Chapter we look at ways in which legal aid can be obtained for inquests.

9.2 The effect of the Legal Aid, Sentencing and Punishment of Offenders Act ("LASPO")

LASPO removed virtually all legal aid for prisoners, except direct release parole hearings and prison disciplinary hearings. However, three areas of legal aid were re-instated in February 2018 after a successful legal challenge brought by the Howard League and the Prisoners' Advice Service, which both provide free legal advice for prisoners. The government has conceded that legal aid can be available for other types of cases. Full details can be found on the Howard League's website at :-

https://howardleague.org/legal-work/legal-aid-cuts-for-prisoners/

Personal injury claims in general came out of the scope of legal aid, following the 2012 Act.

The 2012 Act is sometimes difficult to understand. What it does is define a series of category of case that would normally be excluded from the scope of legal aid, but then it proceeds to say that certain categories are excepted from that exclusion. Very broadly speaking, this means that legal aid is still available for certain categories of litigation case, which include "Abuse of position or powers by public authority" which would include an assault by a prisoner officer.

Schedule 1 Part 1 of LASPO defines precisely what kind of "civil legal services" i.e. legal work done in the civil courts will be covered by legal aid. Paragraph 3 of Schedule 1 Part 1 covers the abuse of a child or a "vulnerable adult". Paragraph 3(5) says that "vulnerable adult" means a person aged 18 or over whose ability to protect himself or herself from abuse is significantly impaired through physical or mental disability or illness, through old age or otherwise. Plainly that could include a serving prisoner with a mental illness. Paragraph 19 covers judicial review, Paragraph 21 "Abuse of position or powers by public authority", Paragraph 22, "Breach of Convention rights by public authority". Paragraph 23 relates to clinical negligence, but this is specifically limited to birth injury cases and it is otherwise excluded from the other paragraphs, Paragraph 39 sexual offences and Paragraph 41 inquests.

Each of these Paragraphs then refers to Schedule 1 Part 2, which contains a list of various types of legal work that would normally be excluded from legal aid. However, Part 2 then says that certain items on this list (and other types of work) are still included within the scope of legal aid. In other words, the exclusions are "excepted" or brought back into scope.

"Abuse of position or powers by public authority" comes under Paragraph 21 of Schedule 1 Part 1 and it is defined as "Civil legal services provided in relation to abuse by a public authority of its position or powers." The "excepted exclusions" are similar to those above for the abuse of a child or vulnerable adult, but they are not exactly the same :-

- The exclusions in Part 2 of Schedule 1, with the exception of paragraphs 1, 2, 3, 4, 5, 6, 8 and 12 of that Part.

- The exclusion in Part 3 of Schedule 1 – essentially advocacy is excepted from this exclusion.
- Clinical negligence.

Part 2 of Schedule 1 sets out the exclusions. Once again, the reader needs to bear in mind that it is the exceptions set out in Part 1 that follow this list, which define what is capable of being legally aided.

> *"1 Civil legal services provided in relation to personal injury or death.*
>
> *2 Civil legal services provided in relation to a claim in tort in respect of negligence.*
>
> *3 Civil legal services provided in relation to a claim in tort in respect of assault, battery or false imprisonment.*
>
> *4 Civil legal services provided in relation to a claim in tort in respect of trespass to goods.*
>
> *5 Civil legal services provided in relation to a claim in tort in respect of trespass to land.*
>
> *6 Civil legal services provided in relation to damage to property.*
>
> *7 Civil legal services provided in relation to defamation or malicious falsehood.*
>
> *8 Civil legal services provided in relation to a claim in tort in respect of breach of statutory duty.*
>
> *9 Civil legal services provided in relation to conveyancing.*
>
> *10 Civil legal services provided in relation to the making of wills.*
>
> *11 Civil legal services provided in relation to matters of trust law."*
>
> *12 [human rights]"*

For the purposes of injuries sustained in prison, the important Paragraphs are Paragraphs 1 to 3, as well as 12.

In relation to Paragraph 3 – abuse of a child or vulnerable adult, the exceptions (i.e. those services that will be covered by legal aid) are found in paragraphs 1, 2, 3, 8 and 12. Consequently, actions brought for negligence, assault, battery, false imprisonment, breach of statutory duty and human rights will qualify for legal aid provided they relate to the abuse of a vulnerable child or adult.

In relation to "Abuse of position or powers by public authority", the exceptions are found paragraphs 1, 2, 3, 4, 5, 6, 8 and 12. Consequently, negligence, assault, battery, false imprisonment, trespass to goods and land, defamation and falsehood, damages to property, breach of statutory duty and human rights will qualify for legal aid provided they relate to abuse by a public authority of its position or powers.

The other Paragraphs to Schedule 1 which might conceivably include a prisoner's claim include similar exceptions.

In relation to Inquests, Paragraph 41 excludes all the services in Schedule 1 Part 2, save for paragraph 1, which includes civil legal services provided in relation to personal injury or death.

9.3 The Legal Aid Regulations

The two main sets of regulations made under LASPO set out the way in which legal aid is granted. These are :-

- The Civil Legal Aid (Merits Criteria) Regulations 2013 (as amended), which are relevant to this discussion. We call these the "Merits Regulations".

- The Civil Legal Aid (Procedure) Regulations 2012, which make provision about the making and withdrawal of determinations that an individual qualifies for civil legal services.

Regulation 4 onwards of the Merits Regulations set out how these criteria (value, costs and success) work.

Regulation 4 states :-

> *"4.—(1) In these Regulations, "prospects of success" means the likelihood that an individual who has made an application for civil legal services will obtain a successful outcome at a trial or other final hearing."*

Regulation 5 then sets out the different prospects i.e. "very good" 80% plus, "good" 60% to 80% and so on.

The 2013 Regulations were amended by the Civil Legal Aid (Merits Criteria) (Amendment) Regulations 2016. The effect of the amendment is that in cases where an application for full legal representation is subject to an assessment of its prospects of success, a case must in general have 50% or higher prospects of success to receive legal aid. In addition, the Legal Aid Agency must fund certain cases that are assessed to have prospects of success that are "borderline" or just below 50% (a 45% or more chance, but less than a 50% chance, defined as "marginal" prospects of success).

Regulation 6 then sets out the definition of "significant wider public interest". A case with significant wider public interest may escape the normal costs benefits rule. However, it will be an extremely rare case that meets the criteria of "significant wider public interest."

Regulation 7 sets out the "reasonable private paying individual test".

> *"For the purposes of these Regulations, the reasonable private paying individual test is met if the Director is satisfied that the potential benefit to be gained from the provision of civil legal services justifies the likely costs, such that a reasonable private paying individual would be prepared to start or continue the proceedings having regard to the prospects of success and all the other circumstances of the case"*

Regulation 8 sets out the "proportionality" test.

> *"8. For the purposes of these Regulations, the proportionality test is met if the Director is satisfied that the likely benefits of the proceedings to the individual and others justify the likely costs, having regard to the prospects of success and all the other circumstances of the case."*

Regulations 9 and 10 define "likely costs" and "likely damages". The legal aided person's likely costs are calculated at legal aid rates (i.e. in London £79.50 per hour), not at the *inter partes* rates that a Claimant would recover if their case was successful.

Briefly there are two types of legal aid available to a person with a litigation case against a public authority, legal help and legal representation. Legal help is generally used as a preliminary form of assistance. It covers the initial work done on the case, but it cannot be used for work that involves actually issuing proceedings or going to court. Consequently, a person wanting to litigate will be signed up on legal help for the first few hours of the case, and then an application will be made for legal representation, in other words a legal aid certificate.

In relation to legal help, Regulation 32 says :-

> *"32. An individual may qualify for legal help only if the Director is satisfied that the following criteria are met—*
>
> *(a) it is reasonable for the individual to be provided with legal help, having regard to any potential sources of funding for the individual other than under Part 1 of the Act; and*
>
> *(b) there is likely to be sufficient benefit to the individual, having regard to all the circumstances of the case, including the circumstances of the individual, to justify the cost of provision of legal help."*

Regulation 39 deals with legal representation. Legal representation may be provided as either investigative representation or full representation.

"39. An individual may qualify for legal representation only if the Director is satisfied that the following criteria are met—

(a) the individual does not have access to other potential sources of funding (other than a conditional fee agreement) from which it would be reasonable to fund the case;

(b) the case is unsuitable for a conditional fee agreement;

(c) there is no person other than the individual, including a person who might benefit from the proceedings, who can reasonably be expected to bring the proceedings;

(d) the individual has exhausted all reasonable alternatives to bringing proceedings including any complaints system, ombudsman scheme or other form of alternative dispute resolution;

(e) there is a need for representation in all the circumstances of the case including—

(i) the nature and complexity of the issues;

(ii) the existence of other proceedings; and

(iii) the interests of other parties to the proceedings; and

(f) the proceedings are not likely to be allocated to the small claims track."

This regulation poses a problem for a legal aid application based on an injury in prison. As we will see below from the Lord Chancellor's Guidance, the Legal Aid Agency will expect firms to run claims on conditional fee agreements in cases where previously the Claimant would have qualified for legal aid.

Regulation 40 sets out the criteria for investigative representation. This is a type of representation used, in effect, to investigate the case, establish its prospects of success at which point full representation may be granted.

Regulation 41 states :-

> *"41. An individual may qualify for full representation only if the Director is satisfied that the criteria in regulation 39 (standard criteria for determinations for legal representation) and the following criteria are met—*
>
> *(a) the cost benefit criteria in regulation 42;*
>
> *(b) the prospects of success criterion in regulation 43; …."*

Regulation 42 sets out the cost benefit criteria.

> *"42.—(1) The cost benefit criteria are as follows.*
>
> *(2) If the case is primarily a claim for damages or other sum of money and is not of significant wider public interest—*
>
> *(a) if the prospects of success of the case are very good, the Director must be satisfied that the likely damages exceed likely costs;*
>
> *(b) if the prospects of success of the case are good, the Director must be satisfied that the likely damages exceed likely costs by a ratio of two to one; or*
>
> *(c) if the prospects of success of the case are moderate, the Director must be satisfied that the likely damages exceed likely costs by a ratio of four to one.*
>
> *(3) If the case is—*
>
> *(a) not primarily a claim for damages or other sum of money; and*
>
> *(b) not of significant wider public interest,*
>
> *the Director must be satisfied that the reasonable private paying individual test is met.*

> *(4) If the case is of significant wider public interest, the Director must be satisfied that the proportionality test is met."*

It is apparent from this Regulation that the solicitor acting for a legally aided Claimant (where these criteria apply) has to apply a strict mathematical formula at the outset of the case. The application for legal aid requires just that. At legal aid rates (in London) of £79.50 per hour, it might be possible run a very good case all the way to trial for less than £25,000 plus VAT. Problems begin when the case is simply "good" in which case if the claim is only worth £15,000 then costs can be no more than half that amount – £7,500. However, because Regulation 10(1)(b) says "likely costs" could be those at the point where the case settles before trial, it can be argued that because settlement is likely, then the total costs will be only £7,500.

Consequently, a realistic valuation of the case is essential right at the outset of the case. A case that is worth only £30,000 may fail the costs/benefits test at the stage when it needs to go trial, because costs are simply too high.

Regulation 43 states :-

> *"43. The prospects of success criterion is only met if the Director is satisfied that the prospects of success are—*
>
> *(a) very good, good or moderate; or*
>
> *(b) borderline, and the case is—*
>
> *(i) of significant wider public interest; or*
>
> *(ii) a case with overwhelming importance to the individual."*

Once again "significant wider public interest" will only cover a very rare client, as will "overwhelming importance."

Regulation 2 says that a "case with overwhelming importance to the individual" means a case which is not primarily a claim for damages or other sum of money and which relates to one or more of the following —

> *"(a) the life, liberty or physical safety of the individual or a member of that individual's family (an individual is a member of another individual's family if the requirements of section 10(6) are met); or*
>
> *(b) the immediate risk that the individual may become homeless";*

Regulation 6 says that the test of "significant wider public interest" will be met

> *"...if the Director is satisfied that the case is an appropriate case to realise –*
>
> *(a) real benefits to the public at large, other than those which normally flow from cases of the type in question; and*
>
> *(b) benefits for an identifiable class of individuals, other than the individual to whom civil legal services may be provided or members of that individual's family."*

Part 6 of the regulations then sets out different criteria for different types of cases, for instance mental health. Regulations 57 to 59 set out the relaxation of the standard criteria in relation to certain types of claim listed in Part 1 Schedule 1 of LASPO. These are Paragraph 21 (abuse of position or powers by public authority) or Paragraph 22 (breach of Convention rights by public authority) of Part 1 of Schedule 1 to the Act. Note that Paragraph 3 in Part 1 Schedule 1 of LASPO – abuse of a child or vulnerable adult – is not covered by the standard criteria.

We now consider the precise effect of Regulations 57 to 59, because for the purposes of this discussion, the relaxation of the normal criteria (for instance the costs/benefits rules) affects the way in which a legal aid application for abuse of position or powers by public authority or a human rights breach, would be assessed.

Regulation 57 relates to investigative representation. This says that in relation to Paragraph 21 (abuse of position or powers by public authority) and Paragraph 22 (human rights) cases, Regulation 39 will apply. This is the regulation that says that when the Applicant applies for legal aid, the Legal Aid Agency must be satisfied that there is no alternative funding available i.e. a conditional fee agreement.

Regulation 58 relates to full representation. This says that in relation to Paragraph 21 (abuse of position or powers by public authority) and Paragraph 22 (human rights) cases, Regulation 39 will apply but the following regulations do not apply. These are Regulations 41(a) and (b), 42 and 43, which are the regulations about costs/benefit and prospects of success.

Instead Regulation 58 prescribes a different type of test. It says :-

> *"An individual may qualify for full representation in relation to any matter described in paragraph 21 (abuse of position or powers by public authority) or 22 (breach of Convention rights by public authority) of Part 1 of Schedule 1 to the Act only if the Director is satisfied that—*
>
> *(a) the proportionality test is met; and*
>
> *(b) the criterion in paragraph (3) is met.*
>
> *(3) The Director must be satisfied that the prospects of success are—*
>
> *(a) very good, good or moderate; or*
>
> *(b) borderline, and—*
>
> *(i) the case is of significant wider public interest;*
>
> *(ii) the case is one with overwhelming importance to the individual; or*

(iii) the substance of the case relates to a breach of Convention rights."

The proportionality test is defined in Regulation 8 as :-

"8. For the purposes of these Regulations, the proportionality test is met if the Director is satisfied that the likely benefits of the proceedings to the individual and others justify the likely costs, having regard to the prospects of success and all the other circumstances of the case."

9.4 The Lord Chancellor's Guidance

The 2013 Regulations run alongside guidance, which is entitled "Lord Chancellor's Guidance under Section 4 of Legal Aid, Sentencing, Punishment of Offenders Act 2012". The Legal Aid Agency must have regard to this guidance in determining whether civil legal services are to be made available under Section 11(1) of the LASPO.

Paragraph 7.12 onwards of the Guidance explains how Regulation 39 of the Merits Regulations work. Paragraph 7.17 has this to say about the suitability of a conditional fee agreement in a case that might qualify for legal aid.

"7.17 The test of unsuitability for a CFA is an objective one, rather than a question of whether an individual provider is willing to act under a CFA (although the test cannot be met if there is evidence of a CFA in fact having been offered or put in place for the applicant). In principle a non-family case may be considered suitable for a conditional fee agreement if: Prospects of success are considered at least at 60% The opponent is considered able to meet any costs and/or damages (or other sum of money) that might be awarded After-the-event insurance can be obtained by the applicant.

7.18 An applicant without after-the-event insurance seeking services otherwise considered suitable for a CFA will be expected to provide evidence of attempts to secure such insurance. Even where evidence is provided of refusals of insurance, the Director him/herself may make enquiries of insurers to see if they would support a CFA in the individual circumstances. Moreover, it will not always be sufficient for the applicant to allege that s/he cannot afford the after-the-event premium. If the proposed claim is for damages then the applicant would need to demonstrate that it has not been possible to defer payment of the premium from any damages recovered.

7.19 If the proposed proceedings do not include a claim for damages or other money, however, particular considerations apply. An applicant for legal aid is unlikely to be able to pay an after-the-event premium or success fee from his/her own resources, and the case should not generally be considered as suitable for a CFA unless both: the prospects of success are at least 80%, (otherwise it would be unreasonable to expect the legal representative to act at risk in relation to costs without the prospect of a success fee or for the applicant to risk an adverse costs order); and the case will not involve significant expenditure on disbursements (in particular experts' fees). Of course, if there is no likelihood of either damages or costs being awarded (for instance in seeking an injunction against an impecunious opponent) then there is no basis on which the case could be pursued under a CFA.

7.20 The fact that the applicant may wish to obtain legal aid rather than a CFA because of the potential deduction from damages in respect of a success premium or damages agreement and/or after-the-event insurance premium, will not of itself prevent a case being suitable for a CFA. The test is not whether the applicant or provider would prefer legal aid to a CFA, but is, in essence, whether the case could realistically be brought under a CFA in the absence of legal aid. It will be a question of fact on the individual circumstances of the case whether the need to meet an insurance payment from the likely damages would render the proceedings futile."

These paragraphs are effectively saying that a Claimant with a claim against the Prison Service must (before they apply for legal aid) explain why they cannot proceed under a conditional fee agreement, and they must show that they have tried to obtain legal expenses insurance.

In the writer's experience, legal expenses insurers will cover claims for abuse against public institutions, particularly if they have an agreement with a particular firm of solicitor to insure all their personal injury claims. However, they may draw the line at certain types of claim with elements that are perceived as high risk, such as a group action or one that is solely based on human rights. The disadvantage from the Claimant's point of view of taking out legal expenses insurance is that he will have to pay for the cost of the premium out of his damages, on top of the success fee. This is an argument that the Lord Chancellor's Guidance specifically anticipates at paragraph 7.20 above, and the Guidance makes it quite clear that it is not on its own, enough to secure a grant of legal aid.

9.5 Proportionality

Further guidance on the proportionality test described in Regulation 58 of the Merits Regulations is provided by the Lord Chancellor's Guidance at paragraphs 4.2.7 onwards :-

> *4.2.7 In assessing the test of whether the proportionality test is met in relation to the likely costs particular regard will be had to those matters set out as regards proportionality in CPR 44.3(5) (as in force from 1 April 2013) relevant to a before the event funding decision as opposed to costs assessment, in particular whether the likely costs bear a reasonable relationship to:*
>
> *(a) The sums in issue in the proceedings*
>
> *(b) The value of any non-monetary relief issue in the proceedings*
>
> *(c) Any wider factors involved in the proceedings, such as reputation or public importance*

4.2.8 For cases not possessing Significant Wider Public Interest, the proportionality test is, however, intended as a less stringent test than the prospects of success, damages, costs matrix or the reasonable private paying individual test because of the higher priority of the proceedings to which it is applied. Accordingly, for any claim that is primarily for damages or other sums of money, the proportionality test will be considered to be satisfied pursuant to CPR 44.3(5)(a) if the appropriate damages (or other sums) to costs ratio is met. For other claims the test will be considered satisfied having regard to CPR 44.3(5)(b), if the reasonable private individual test is met.

4.2.9 Otherwise in considering "all the circumstances of the case" in regulation 8 of the merits regulations, it will be necessary to consider (i) the importance of the issues raised by the case pursuant to CPR 44.3(5)(e):, for example how serious is the abuse of power alleged in a claim against a public authority? (ii) how far short of the appropriate damages/costs ratio or the reasonable private paying individual the case falls. The less cost effective the case appears to be, the more serious must be the issues raised by the case to justify the provision of services."

9.6 Funding for Inquests

The Inquest Newsletter for 14 March – 29 April 2019 has a report on a recent debate on legal aid for inquests in parliament.

In relation to Inquests, Paragraph 41(1) of Schedule 1 Part 1 LASPO includes within the scope of legal aid *"Civil legal services provided to an individual in relation to an inquest under the Coroners Act 1988 into the death of a member of the individual's family."*

However, Paragraph 41(2)(a) says that all of the services that can be provided under Schedule 1 Part 2 are excluded with the sole exception of Paragraph 1 Part 2 which is "Civil legal services provided in relation to personal injury or death." Paragraph 2 – civil legal services provided in relation to a claim in tort in respect of negligence, Paragraph 3 – civil legal services provided in relation to a claim in tort in respect of assault, battery or false imprisonment are not included and Paragraph 12 – human rights are not included. It is not clear whether the effect of the above would prevent a legally aided Claimant with a personal injury claim based on Paragraphs 2,3 or 12 Part 2, from using that certificate to fund the costs of an inquest. If the certificate did not cover that work, then a successful Claimant might have difficulty recovering his litigation costs against the Prison Service. As the law stands, a Defendant can object to paying inquest costs although they may be recoverable – see ***Douglas v Ministry of Justice & Anor [2018] EWHC B2 (Costs).***

There is a further exclusion to Paragraph 41. Paragraph 41(2)(b) says that any civil legal services provided in connection with an inquest are subject to the exclusion in Part 3 of Schedule 1. This Part deals with advocacy and it sets out the types of court and tribunal, where legal aid is granted. These courts include the High Court and the County Court as well as the appellate courts, but the Coroners' Courts are not included. The absence of legal aid cover for advocacy before the Coroner effectively rules out funding for the most important part of the process.

However, as the government's own website points out, Section 10 of LASPO gives the Legal Aid Agency to grant legal aid even though the work to be done is outside the scope of legal aid. The relevant website page can be found at :-

https://www.gov.uk/guidance/legal-aid-apply-for-exceptional-case-funding

This type of legal aid is known as Exceptional Case Funding ("ECF") and it covers both inquest and non-inquest work. The website address above provides a link to a document published by the Legal Aid Agency entitled "Lord Chancellor's Exceptional Funding Guidance (Inquests)". The guidance begins by saying that the Government has retained Legal Help, the advice and assistance level of legal aid, for inquests into the death of a member of the individual's family. Legal Help can cover all of the preparatory work associated with the inquest, which may include preparing written submissions to the Coroner.

The guidance says that there are two grounds for granting legal aid for representation at an inquest. The first is that the representation is required by Article 2 of the European Convention on Human Rights. The second is where the Director makes a "wider public interest determination" in relation to the individual and the inquest.

In relation to the first ground, the guidance states that it is unlikely that there will be an arguable breach of Article 2 where there is no State involvement in the death, or where the death took place in State detention through natural causes or where the case involved only allegations of ordinary clinical negligence.

In relation to the second ground "wider public interest" determination, the guidance says that this would mean an inquest that was likely to produce significant benefits for a class of person, other than the applicant and members of the applicant's family. In the context of an inquest, the most likely wider public benefits are the identification of dangerous practices, systematic failings or other findings that identify significant risks to the life, health or safety of other persons. The "wider public interest" must be "significant".

Paragraphs 17 and 33 of the guidance indicate that the Coroner's view on these issues may be taken into account. For this reason, it is recommended to approach the Coroner and seek his views on either or both of the two grounds, which he should be invited to do in a letter to the Legal Aid Agency.

In general applicants must satisfy the eligibility (i.e. means test) limits. However, there is a discretion to waive the financial eligibility limits relating to inquests if, in all the circumstances, it would not be reasonable to expect the applicant to bear the full costs of legal assistance at the inquest.

CHAPTER TEN
COMPLAINTS ABOUT PRISONS

10.1 The statutory system

Regulation 11 of the Prison Rules 1999 says that a prisoner may make a request or complaint to their relevant governor or independent monitoring board. The governor of the prison shall consider that complaint as soon as possible. A written complaint is confidential.

Regulation 78(1) says that the independent monitoring board for a prison and any member of the board shall hear any complaint or request, which a prisoner wishes to make to them.

Regulation 8 of the Young Offender Institution Rules 2000 and Regulation 8 of the Secure Training Centre Rules 1998 contains the same rights to make a complaint for those types of institution.

Children in Secure Accommodation would normally make a complaint, under the Children Act 1989 complaints system, to the local authority, which runs the unit.

10.2 Prison Service Instruction 02/2012

The complaints procedure for all prisons, Youth Offender Institutions and Secure Training Centres are contained within a document entitled Prison Service Instruction (PSI) 02/2012. This can be found at https://www.justice.gov.uk/offenders/psis/prison-service-instructions-2012. This PSI expires on the 1st December 2016 but it appears to the most up to date procedure.

PSI 02/2012 sets out a two stage complaints process.

Complaint forms (which are prescribed under PSI 02/2012) must be made freely available to prisoners. Prisoners must be informed about the complaint procedures during the "early days" of their time in custody.

Complaints will normally be made in writing and processed on working days only, although prisons must have arrangements in place to enable urgent complaints to be considered on non-working days.

Prisons must have arrangements in place, which will allow a prisoner to make a formal complaint orally to a member of staff where the prisoner has difficulty doing so in writing. In such circumstances, the complaint must be recorded and the written answer must be explained to the prisoner in due course.

Complaints should normally be submitted within three months of the incident or circumstances which give rise to the complaint, or the date on which they became known to the prisoner. Prisoners must receive a response to their complaint within 5 working days of the complaint being logged.

If a prisoner is dissatisfied with the response to his or her complaint, they may resubmit the complaint using an appeal form, setting out the reasons why. An appeal should normally be made within 7 calendar days of the prisoner having received the initial response, unless there are exceptional reasons why this would have been difficult or impossible. The appeal form should be submitted in the same way as the original complaint form. Prisoners must receive a response to their appeal within 5 working days of the appeal being logged.

Appeals must be answered by someone at a higher level in the management structure than the person who provided the response to the original complaint.

The time limits can vary depending on the type of complaint made. Annex B to PSI 02/2012 sets out those time limits.

If the prisoner is dissatisfied with the appeal process, they can approach the Prisons and Probation Ombudsman.

10.3 Probation Instructions 51/2014 – The Complaints System for People on Probation

The predecessor to the Her Majesty's Prison and Probation Service, the National Offender Management Service, published a Probation Standard Complaints Procedure under reference PI 51/2014. This sets out the government's "Probation Instructions" on the complaints system to be operated by the National Probation Service and Community Rehabilitation Companies.

Once again, this is recommended reading for anyone who is submitting a complaint, about the delivery of probation services, to the National Probation Service or a Community Rehabilitation Company.

The scheme can be found at :-

www.justice.gov.uk/offenders/probation-instructions

10.4 The Prisons and Probation Ombudsman ("PPO")

The PPO's website can be found at :- www.ppo.gov.uk.

The PPO sets out its terms of reference at :- www.ppo.gov.uk/about/vision-and-values/terms-of-reference. This is not a particularly long document and is recommended reading for anyone wishing to approach the PPO.

The PPO has two main duties :-

- To investigate complaints made by prisoners, young people in detention (prisons and secure training centres), offenders under probation supervision, and immigration detainees.

- To investigate deaths of prisoners, young people in detention, approved premises' residents, and immigration detainees due to any cause, including any apparent suicides and natural causes.

The PPO will investigate fatal incidents in Secure Children's Homes or Secure Accommodation but not complaints from children and young people in these types of homes. These kinds of complaints can be brought under the procedures laid down in the Children's Homes (England) Regulations 2015.

Before putting a complaint to the PPO, a complainant must first seek redress through appropriate use of the relevant prison, youth detention accommodation, probation, or Home Office complaints procedure.

Complainants submitting their case to the PPO must do so within three calendar months of receiving a substantive reply in the internal complaint procedure. The PPO will not normally accept complaints where there has been a delay of more than 12 months between the complainant becoming aware of the relevant facts and submitting their case to the PPO, unless the delay has been the fault of the relevant authority and the PPO considers that it is appropriate to do so. The PPO has discretion to investigate those complaints where it considers there to be good reason for the delay, or where it considers the issues raised to be of sufficient severity to make an exception to the usual timeframe.

Once it has accepted the complaint, the PPO will undertake an investigation.

Fatalities are investigated by the Fatal Incidents Teams.

The PPO has an extensive archive of Fatal Incident Reports on their website as well as report on incidents in various prisons.

The PPO cannot investigate :-

- the clinical judgement of medical professionals

- policy decisions taken by a Minister of State
- cases currently the subject of civil litigation or criminal proceedings
- conviction, sentence, immigration status, reasons for immigration detention or the length of such detentions
- decisions or recommendations of the judiciary, the police, the Crown Prosecution Service and the Parole Board

Many prisoners suffer from medical problems and there are often questions as to the standard of their medical care. Whilst the PPO cannot investigate a medical decision, their investigation can include examining the clinical issues relevant to each death. In the case of deaths in prisons, youth detention accommodation, Secure Children's Homes, and immigration facilities, the PPO will ask NHS England to review the clinical care and examine the question of whether referrals to secondary healthcare were made appropriately.

Obviously, PPO decisions can be extremely helpful in terms of framing a civil action.

A complainant who is dissatisfied with the way the PPO has dealt with his or her case can write a letter to request a review. The investigation will be reviewed by a member of senior staff who has not been involved in the case before. If there is some dispute about the failure to adequately investigate and the PPO closes their file, then the complainant is able to request that their MP refer the case to the Parliamentary and Health Service Ombudsman. For more information about the PHSO see their website www.ombudsman.org.uk.

MORE BOOKS BY LAW BRIEF PUBLISHING

A selection of our other titles available now:-

'A Practical Guide to TOLATA Claims' by Greg Williams
'Planning Obligations Demystified: A Practical Guide to Planning Obligations and Section 106 Agreements' by Bob Mc Geady & Meyric Lewis
'A Practical Guide to Agricultural Law and Tenancies' by Christopher McNall
'A Practical Guide to Crofting Law' by Brian Inkster
'A Practical Guide to Spousal Maintenance' by Liz Cowell
'A Practical Guide to the Law of Domain Names and Cybersquatting' by Andrew Clemson
'A Practical Guide to the Law of Gender Pay Gap Reporting' by Harini Iyengar
'Ellis and Kevan on Credit Hire – 5th Edition' by Aidan Ellis & Tim Kevan
'Artificial Intelligence – The Practical Legal Issues' by John Buyers
'A Practical Guide to the Rights of Grandparents in Children Proceedings' by Stuart Barlow
'NHS Whistleblowing and the Law' by Joseph England
'Employment Law and the Gig Economy' by Nigel Mackay & Annie Powell
'A Practical Guide to the General Data Protection Regulation (GDPR)' by Keith Markham
'A Practical Guide to Noise Induced Hearing Loss (NIHL) Claims' by Andrew Mckie, Ian Skeate, Gareth McAloon
'An Introduction to Beauty Negligence Claims – A Practical Guide for the Personal Injury Practitioner' by Greg Almond
'Intercompany Agreements for Transfer Pricing Compliance' by Paul Sutton
'Zen and the Art of Mediation' by Martin Plowman
'A Practical Guide to the SRA Principles, Individual and Law Firm Codes of Conduct 2019 – What Every Law Firm Needs to Know' by Paul Bennett

'A Practical Guide to Licensing Law for Commercial Property Lawyers' by Niall McCann & Richard Williams
'A Practical Guide to Adoption for Family Lawyers' by Graham Pegg
'Essential Motor Finance Law for the Busy Practitioner' by Richard Humphreys
'A Practical Guide to Industrial Disease Claims' by Andrew Mckie & Ian Skeate
'A Practical Guide to the Law of Armed Conflict' by Jo Morris & Libby Anderson
'A Practical Guide to Redundancy' by Philip Hyland
'A Practical Guide to Vicarious Liability' by Mariel Irvine
'A Practical Guide to Claims Arising from Delays in Diagnosing Cancer' by Bella Webb
'A Practical Guide to Applications for Landlord's Consent and Variation of Leases' by Mark Shelton
'A Practical Guide to Relief from Sanctions Post-Mitchell and Denton' by Peter Causton
'Butler's Equine Tax Planning: 2nd Edition' by Julie Butler
'A Practical Guide to Equity Release for Advisors' by Paul Sams
'A Practical Guide to Unlawful Eviction and Harassment' by Stephanie Lovegrove
'A Practical Guide to the Law Relating to Food' by Ian Thomas
'A Practical Guide to the Ending of Assured Shorthold Tenancies' by Elizabeth Dwomoh
'A Practical Guide to Financial Services Claims' by Chris Hegarty
'The Law of Houses in Multiple Occupation: A Practical Guide to HMO Proceedings' by Julian Hunt
'A Practical Guide to Unlawful Eviction and Harassment' by Stephanie Lovegrove
'A Practical Guide to Solicitor and Client Costs' by Robin Dunne
'A Practical Guide to Wrongful Conception, Wrongful Birth and Wrongful Life Claims' by Rebecca Greenstreet
'Occupiers, Highways and Defective Premises Claims: A Practical Guide Post-Jackson – 2nd Edition' by Andrew Mckie
'A Practical Guide to Financial Ombudsman Service Claims' by Adam Temple & Robert Scrivenor

‘A Practical Guide to the Law of Enfranchisement and Lease Extension’
by Paul Sams

‘A Practical Guide to Marketing for Lawyers – 2nd Edition’
by Catherine Bailey & Jennet Ingram

'A Practical Guide to Advising Schools on Employment Law' by Jonathan Holden

'Certificates of Lawful Use and Development: A Guide to Making and Determining Applications' by Bob Mc Geady & Meyric Lewis

'A Practical Guide to the Law of Dilapidations' by Mark Shelton

‘A Practical Guide to the 2018 Jackson Personal Injury and Costs Reforms’
by Andrew Mckie

‘A Guide to Consent in Clinical Negligence Post-Montgomery’
by Lauren Sutherland QC

‘A Practical Guide to Running Housing Disrepair and Cavity Wall Claims: 2nd Edition’ by Andrew Mckie & Ian Skeate

‘A Practical Guide to Digital and Social Media Law for Lawyers’ by Sherree Westell

‘A Practical Guide to Holiday Sickness Claims – 2nd Edition’
by Andrew Mckie & Ian Skeate

‘A Practical Guide to Elderly Law’ by Justin Patten

‘Arguments and Tactics for Personal Injury and Clinical Negligence Claims’
by Dorian Williams

‘A Practical Guide to QOCS and Fundamental Dishonesty’ by James Bentley

‘A Practical Guide to Drone Law’ by Rufus Ballaster, Andrew Firman, Eleanor Clot

‘Practical Mediation: A Guide for Mediators, Advocates, Advisers, Lawyers, and Students in Civil, Commercial, Business, Property, Workplace, and Employment Cases’ by Jonathan Dingle with John Sephton

‘A Comparative Guide to Standard Form Construction and Engineering Contracts’
by Jon Close

‘A Practical Guide to Compliance for Personal Injury Firms Working With Claims Management Companies’ by Paul Bennett

‘A Practical Guide to the Landlord and Tenant Act 1954: Commercial Tenancies’
by Richard Hayes & David Sawtell

‘A Practical Guide to Psychiatric Claims in Personal Injury’ by Liam Ryan

‘A Practical Guide to Dog Law for Owners and Others’ by Andrea Pitt

www.ingramcontent.com/pod-product-compliance
Lightning Source LLC
LaVergne TN
LVHW022054200926
848481LV00003B/904